Great Meals in Minutes

Vegetable Menus

Great Meals in Minutes was created by Rebus Inc., and published by Time-Life Books.

This edition published 1994 by Bloomsbury Books, an imprint of The Godfrey Cave Group, 42 Bloomsbury Street, London, WC1B 3QJ.

© 1994 Time-Life Books BV.

ISBN 1 85471 581 X

Printed and bound in Great Britain.

Vegetable Menus

Madhur Jaffrey
Menu 1
Rice Pilaf with Black-Eyed Peas — 8
Eggplant in Spicy Tomato Sauce

Menu 2
Persian-Style Rice with Lima Beans and Dill — 10
Cauliflower with Garlic and Sesame Seeds
Yogurt with Tomato and Cucumber

Menu 3
Brown Rice with Mushrooms — 12
Peas and Tomatoes with Cumin Seeds
Yogurt with Mint

Marlene Sorosky
Menu 1
Chicken in Parchment with Mushrooms
    and Tomatoes — 16
Green Salad with Fried Goat Cheese

Menu 2
Deep-Dish Vegetable Pot Pies — 18
Fresh Orange and Green Salad

Menu 3
Spaghetti Squash with Garden Vegetable Sauce — 21
Almond Popovers with Ameretto Butter

Beverly Cox
Menu 1
Eggplant Pie — 26
Green Bean and Onion Salad
Oranges with Cinnamon

Menu 2
Louisiana-Style Mirlitons Stuffed with Ham
    and Shrimp — 28
Marinated Carrots

Menu 3
Chicken Breasts with a Bouquet of Vegetables
    and Sweet-and Sour Sauce — 30
Green Salad with Herbed Vinaigrette

Jane Salzfass Freiman
Menu 1
Seafood Salad — 36
Cheese and Scallion Enchiladas with Guacamole Sauce

Menu 2
Watercress Soup — 38
Grilled Cod with Red-Pepper Sauce
Steamed New Potatoes

Menu 3
Pasta with Fresh Mushroom Sauce — 40
Boston Lettuce, Fennel, and Radicchio Salad

Martha Rose Shulman
Menu 1
Saffron Millet — 44
Stir-Fried Tofu with Snow Peas
Hot-and-Sour Cucumber Salad

Menu 2
Chilies con Queso — 46
Spanish Rice
Guacamole Chalupas

Menu 3
Puffed Broccoli Omlettes — 49
Wild Rice with Almonds
Curried Pumpkin Purée

Peter Kump
Menu 1
Beetroot Salad/Tomato Salad/Carrot Salad — 54
Turkey Scallops with Brown Butter and Caper Sauce
Green Beans with Sweet-and-Sour Sauce

Menu 2
Celeriac Winter Salad — 56
Chicken Piccata
Braised Fresh Spinach and Mushrooms

Menu 3
Cream of Lemon Soup — 58
Fillets of Sole with Courgettes and Peppers
Blueberry Cream-Cheese Parfaits

Bloomsbury Books
London

Madhur Jaffrey

Menu 1
(*Right*)
Rice Pilaf with Black-Eyed Peas
and Green Beans
Eggplant in Spicy Tomato Sauce

Cooking with vegetables and grains is an observance of Hindu religious tradition, which reveres all animal life. Madhur Jaffrey, who is an actress as well as a food writer and cook, learned vegetable cookery in her native India. Vegetables please her spirit and sustain her, she explains. Her three menus guide those who want vegetarian meals that are authentic, simple, and nutritionally balanced. At the heart of Indian cooking is rice – the main dish in each of these menus. As accompaniments, Madhur Jaffrey serves eggplant in a tomato sauce in Menu 1, seasoned cauliflower and a chilled, yogurt-based salad in Menu 2, and a bright mixture of peas and tomatoes along with a minty yogurt in Menu 3.

Like the best Indian cooks, Madhur Jaffrey prepares her vegetables to underscore their natural essence rather than to make them look and taste like meat. She balances her vegetarian meals with nuts, yogurt, and fruits – only a few of the elements in the almost endlessly rich and varied repertoire of Indian cooking – and adds dimension to her recipes by using spices and seasonings, such as whole or ground cumin and coriander seeds, which are an integral part of the cuisine.

The main dish in this festive, all-vegetable Indian meal is rice pilaf with black-eyed peas and green beans, accompanied by a casserole of broiled sliced eggplant in a spicy tomato sauce.

Rice Pilaf with Black-Eyed Peas and Green Beans
Eggplant in Spicy Tomato Sauce

India is famous for rice pilaf, which is rice fried and then braised with vegetables and seasonings. Here Madhur Jaffrey mixes the rice with black-eyed peas and green beans and serves a fennel-flavoured eggplant dish on the side.

Frozen black-eyed peas are almost as good as fresh ones and much easier to handle. If you want to use dried peas, you must cook them ahead: Prick through the dried peas to remove unwanted particles, then wash them. Set them to simmer in about 7¹/₂ cm (3 inches) of water in a large pot. After 2 minutes of simmering, turn the heat off, cover the pot, and let the peas sit for an hour. Then cook them 10 to 20 minutes.

Tumeric, a bright yellow spice in the ginger family, is common on American supermarket shelves, but you may need to shop for whole cumin, coriander, and fennel seeds in a speciality shop or Indian grocery. Fennel seeds have a pleasant, mild licorice taste, like anise, which you can substitute if you reduce the quantity. Frying spices, as in this recipe, helps release and intensify their flavour.

Eggplant soaks up oil when you fry it so broiling the slices with a light brushing of oil cuts down on fat.

Broiling also helps eliminate the sometimes bitter taste of eggplant skin. The cook recommends white eggplant for this recipe, or the small Oriental eggplants, but you can use any of the several varieties you may find at the greengrocer.

The tomato sauce for the eggplant slices calls for coarsely chopped fresh ginger. The cook's technique for coarse-chopping ginger is to peel a section of fresh ginger and then slice it thinly. Use a potato masher to smash the ginger slices, then drag them across the surface of the cutting board to break up the fibres.

To make this meal nutritionally complete, include a dessert of fresh fruit with a dairy product. This could be either a platter of fruit, accompanied by a selection of various cheeses, or a bowl of peeled and sliced fresh fruit folded into sweetened yogurt or ice cream.

What to drink

The cook suggests a dry red wine with character, such as an Italian Montepulciano d'Abruzzo, to accompany this lively meal. Cold beer or light ale also would be good.

Start-to-Finish Steps

1 Follow rice pilaf recipe steps 1 through to 3. Squeeze enough lemon to measure 2 tablespoons juice, peel and mince garlic, peel and finely chop onion, trim green beans and cut crosswise into pieces.
2 Follow rice pilaf recipe steps 4 and 5.
3 Drain rice and follow rice pilaf recipe steps 6 and 7.
4 For eggplant recipe, peel and coarsely chop ginger, peel garlic cloves, and chop tomatoes.
5 Follow eggplant recipe steps 1 through 5.
6 Toss rice and serve with the eggplant.

Rice Pilaf with Black-Eyed Peas and Green Beans

350 g (12 oz) long-grain rice, preferably basmati
300 g (10 oz) package frozen black-eyed peas
2 teaspoons ground coriander
1 teaspoon ground cumin
$^1/_2$ teaspoon ground turmeric
$^1/_8$ to $^1/_4$ teaspoon Cayenne pepper
$^1/_4$ teaspoon coarsely ground black pepper
Dash of cinnamon
2 tablespoons lemon juice
4 tablespoons vegetable oil
1 medium-size clove garlic, peeled and minced
1 medium-size onion, peeled and finely chopped
125 g (4 oz) green beans, trimmed and cut crosswise into 1 cm ($^1/_2$ inch) pieces
$1^1/_4$ teaspoons salt

1 Place rice in large bowl with cold water to cover. With your hands, swish the rice around quickly; pour off most of the water. Repeat 6 to 8 times, or until water is no longer cloudy. Cover rice with water; set aside 25 minutes.
2 In medium-size saucepan, bring 350 ml (12 fl oz) of water to a boil. Add black-eyed peas and return to a boil, breaking up frozen block of peas with fork as they are heating. Cover, turn heat to low, and simmer 10 minutes. Drain peas in colander.
3 While peas are cooking, combine coriander, cumin, turmeric, Cayenne, black pepper, cinnamon, lemon juice, and 1 tablespoon of water in small cup. Mix thoroughly and set aside.
4 In large, heavy-gauge saucepan or skillet, heat oil over medium heat. When hot, add garlic and onion. Cook, stirring with wooden spatula, until onion turns brown at edges.
5 Add spice mixture and stir well to combine. Fry about 1 minute.
6 Add the drained rice, black-eyed peas, green beans, and salt. Cook over medium heat 2 to 3 minutes, stirring carefully so as not to break the grains of rice. Lower heat if rice begins to stick to bottom of pan.
7 Add 750 ml ($1^1/_2$ pints) water and bring to a boil. Cover tightly, first with aluminium foil and then with a lid. Turn heat very low and cook 25 minutes. Keep pilaf tightly covered until ready to serve

Eggplant in Spicy Tomato Sauce

1 large eggplant 750 g ($1^1/_2$ lb)
9 tablespoons vegetable oil (approximately)
1 piece fresh ginger $3^1/_2$ x $2^1/_2$ cm ($1^1/_2$ x 1 inch), peeled and coarsely chopped
6 medium-size cloves garlic, peeled
1 teaspoon whole fennel seeds
1 teaspoon whole cumin seeds
3 medium-size tomatoes, chopped
1 tablespoon ground coriander
1 teaspoon salt
$^1/_4$ teaspoon ground turmeric
$^1/_8$ to $^1/_4$ teaspoon Cayenne pepper

1 Preheat broiler.
2 Halve eggplant lengthwise and then cut crosswise into 1 cm ($^1/_2$ inch) slices.
3 Brush slices on both sides with about 3 tablespoons of the oil and arrange them in a single layer in large broiling tray. Broil $7^1/_2$ cm (3 inches) from heat source, about 7 minutes, or until eggplant is nicely browned.
4 While eggplant is broiling, purée ginger, garlic, and 3 tablespoons of water in food processor or blender. Set aside. In large skillet, heat remaining 6 tablespoons of oil over medium heat. When hot, add fennel and cumin seeds, and let sizzle 30 seconds, or until seeds turn a shade darker. Add ginger-garlic purée and cook, stirring, 1 minute. Stir in chopped tomatoes, coriander, salt, tumeric, and Cayenne, and bring to a simmer. Cook, turn heat to low, and cook 5 minutes.
5 Fold the browned eggplant slices into the tomato sauce and bring to a simmer. Cover and cook over low heat another 3 to 5 minutes. Turn into serving dish.

Leftover suggestions

If you have leftover eggplant slices, serve them folded into some lightly fork-beaten plain yogurt. To reheat the rice pilaf, sauté it in hot oil with scallions and serve it as a snack or light lunch.

Persian-Style Rice with Lima Beans and Dill
Cauliflower with Garlic and Sesame Seeds
Yogurt with Tomato and Cucumber

You can buy *basmati* rice in an Indian grocery or speciality food shop; it is aromatic, with delicate, long slender grains. pick through it carefully before rinsing to remove unwanted particles.

The cauliflower recipe calls for unhulled sesame seeds, which you can buy in a health food store or in an Indian or Chinese market. Be sure to sift through the seeds to remove any grit before you use them. A precautionary note: when dropped into hot oil, sesame sedds will pop; have a lid or spatter guard handy to hold them in the skillet.

What to drink

a dry white wine is needed for this menu: a French Mâcon, a California Sauvignon Blanc, or an Italian Chardonnay would all be appropriate choices.

Colourful plates highlight the muted tones of the Persian rice, sautéed cauliflower, and yogurt-vegetable mixture.

Start-to-Finish Steps

1 Follow Persian-style rice recipe step 1.
2 Follow cauliflower recipe step 1.
3 Follow Persian-style rice recipe step 2.
4 Follow yogurt recipe steps 1 through 3. Refrigerate until ready to serve.
5 Drain rice and follow Persian-style rice recipe steps 3 through 4.
6 Trim cauliflower and break into small florets. Follow cauliflower recipe steps 2 through 4.
7 Toss rice and serve with the cauliflower and the yogurt.

Persian-Style Rice with Lima Beans and Dill

350 g (12 oz) long-grain rice, preferably basmati
300 g (10 oz) package frozen baby lima beans
1¼ teaspoons salt
4 tablespoons vegetable oil
1 small onion, peeled and thinly sliced
45 g (1½ oz) firmly packed chopped fresh dill
1½ teaspoons chopped fresh thyme, or ½ teaspoon dried

1 Place rice in large bowl and wash in several changes of water. Drain in colander. Return rice to bowl and cover with 5 cups of water; set aside 25 minutes.
2 While rice is soaking, cook lima beans in small saucepan in ½ cup water with ¼ teaspoon salt for 8 minutes. Drain in colander.
3 In large, heavy-gauge saucepan, heat oil over medium heat. When hot, add onion. Cook, stirring, until onion is lightly browned. Add drained rice, lima beans, dill, thyme, and remaining salt. Stir gently and cook 2 to 3 minutes, taking care not to break the grains of rice. If rice begins to stick to bottom of pan, turn down heat a bit.
4 Pour in 625 ml (1¼ pts) cups of water and bring to a boil. Cover tightly, first with aluminium foil and then with lid. Turn heat to very low and cook 25 minutes. Keep covered until ready to serve.

Cauliflower with Garlic and Sesame Seeds

Salt
1 medium-size cauliflower, broken into small florets
4 tablespoons vegetable oil
4 to 5 cloves garlic, peeled and minced
1½ tablespoons unhulled sesame seeds
Dash Cayenne pepper
Freshly ground black pepper

1 In large, heavy-gauge saucepan, bring 3 ltrs (5 pints) of water to a boil. Stir in 1 tablespoon salt.
2 Add cauliflower and return water to a rolling boil. boil rapidly 1 to 1½ minutes, or until cauliflower is crisply tender. Drain in colander and set aside.
3 In large skillet, heat oil over medium heat. When hot, add garlic. Fry, stirring, until garlic turns light brown.
4 Add sesame seeds. When sesame seeds turn a few shades darker or begin to pop, add the cauliflower. Stir cauliflower gently until evenly coated with sesame seeds. Add Cayenne, a generous amount of black pepper, and about ¼ teaspoon salt, and stir once more. Turn into serving bowl.

Yogurt with Tomato and Cucumber

1 medium-size ripe tomato
1 medium-size cucumber
350 ml (12 fl oz) plain yogurt
½ teaspoon salt
Freshly ground black pepper
Dash Cayenne pepper

1 Core tomato and cut into 5 mm (¼ inch) dice. Peel cucumber and cut into 1 cm (½ inch) dice.
2 Turn yogurt into serving bowl and beat lightly with fork or whisk until smooth and creamy.
3 Add vegetables and seasonings and mix. Taste and adjust seasonings if necessary.

This informal Indian vegetarian meal features brown rice with sliced mushrooms, peas and chopped tomatoes spiced with cumin, and yogurt with chopped mint. Pass the yogurt separately and, if you wish, garnish with sprigs of fresh mint.

Not many Asians eat brown rice. They prefer white because its bland taste does not compete with other savoury ingredients. But brown rice, which is unmilled white rice, has a distinctive nutty flavor that appeals to many Westerners. Madhur Jaffrey prefers the texture of long-grain brown rice, but you can use the short-grain variety. To soften it quickly, soak it for 20 minutes in hot water to cover. Remember that brown rice requires a longer cooking time than white, so plan accordingly. The cooked rice dish can stand for half an hour without being ruined. Just remove the foil and replace it with a clean dish towel, which helps to absorb the extra moisture, and set the lid on top of the towel. You can vary this menu and still keep it balanced by substituting whole wheat pitta bread for the rice recipe.

The combination of seven spices together with peas and tomatoes is a traditional Delhi dish. In Menus 1 and 2, you fry the spices to bring out their taste, but here you mix them with water into a paste before you fry them.

Mint probably came from Turkey originally, but Indians have adopted it universally. Chopped mint and yogurt, stirred together, cool and refresh the palate after a spicy meal.

If you like, serve fresh fruit, such as melon, berries, mangoes, or pineapple, for dessert.

What to drink
The flavours in this menu would blend best with a small, accommodating red wine, such as an Italian Valpolicella or California Pinot Noir.

Start-to-Finish Steps
1 Follow brown rice recipe step 1. Peel and mince garlic, peel and chop onion, clean mushrooms with damp paper towels and slice thinly, and mince enough parsley to measure 2 tablespoons.
2 Follow brown rice recipe steps 2 through 5.
3 For peas and tomatoes recipe, grate enough nutmeg to measure $1/4$ teaspoon, peel and finely chop onion, and core and finely chop tomatoes.
4 Follow peas and tomatoes recipe steps 1 through 7.
5 Prepare yogurt with mint.
6 Toss brown rice and serve with the peas and tomatoes and the yogurt with mint.

Brown Rice with Mushrooms

300 g (10 oz) long-grain brown rice
4 tablespoons vegetable oil
1 clove garlic, peeled and minced
1 small onion, peeled and finely chopped
8 medium-size mushrooms, wiped clean and thinly
    sliced
2 tablespoons minced parsley
1 teaspoon salt

1 Place rice in large bowl and wash in several changes of water. Drain in colander. Return rice to bowl and cover with 750 ml (1¹/₂ pints) of hot water; set aside 20 minutes.
2 In large, heavy-gauge saucepan, heat oil over medium heat. When hot, add garlic and onion. Fry, stirring, until onion turns brown at edges.
3 Stir in mushrooms and fry them until they wilt.
4 Sprinkle parsley over mixture and stir a few seconds.
5 Add rice with its soaking liquid and salt. Bring to a boil. Cover tightly, first with aluminium foil and then with lid. Turn heat down to very low and cook 35 minutes. Turn off heat and let pan sit in warm spot, covered and undisturbed, another 5 minutes.

Peas and Tomatoes with Whole Cumin

2 Kg (4 lb) fresh peas (approximately)
2 teaspoons ground cumin
2 teaspoons ground coriander
¹/₈ to ¹/₄ teaspoon Cayenne pepper
¹/₂ teaspoon ground turmeric
¹/₄ teaspoon coarsely ground black pepper
¹/₄ teaspoon ground ginger
¹/₄ teaspoon freshly grated nutmeg
4 tablespoons vegetable oil
1 teaspoon whole cumin seeds
1 small onion, peeled and finely chopped
3 ripe tomatoes, cored and finely chopped (about
    625 g (1¹/₄ lb) pounds total weight)
1 teaspoon salt
1 teaspoon brown sugar

1 Shell the peas. Set aside.
2 In small cup, mix cumin, coriander, Cayenne, turmeric, black pepper, ginger, and nutmeg with 5 tablespoons warm water, and set aside.
3 In large sauté pan, heat oil over medium heat. When hot, add whole cumin seeds. Sizzle about 20 seconds.

4 Add chopped onion and fry, stirring, until edges begin to brown.
5 Stir in spice paste and fry with the onion 2 minutes.
6 Add tomatoes. Bring to a vigorous simmer over slightly higher heat. Stir and cook 3 to 4 minutes, or until the tomatoes soften and reduce.
7 Stir in peas, salt, and brown sugar. Bring to a simmer. Cover, turn heat to low, and cook 5 minutes, or until peas are just tender. Turn into serving dish.

Yogurt with Mint

350 g (12 fl oz) plain yogurt
¹/₂ to ³/₄ teaspoon salt
Freshly ground black pepper
Dash Cayenne pepper (optional)
3 tablespoons finely chopped mint

Turn yogurt into serving bowl. Beat lightly with fork or whisk until smooth and creamy. Add remaining ingredients and mix well.

Leftover suggestions
Leftover peas and tomatoes become a kind of stew you add 2 boiled beets, peeled and cut into 1 cm (¹/₂ inch) pieces, and some stock or water. Turn the brown rice with mushrooms into a pilaf by heating it in a skillet and adding diced cooked chicken or meat from another meal.

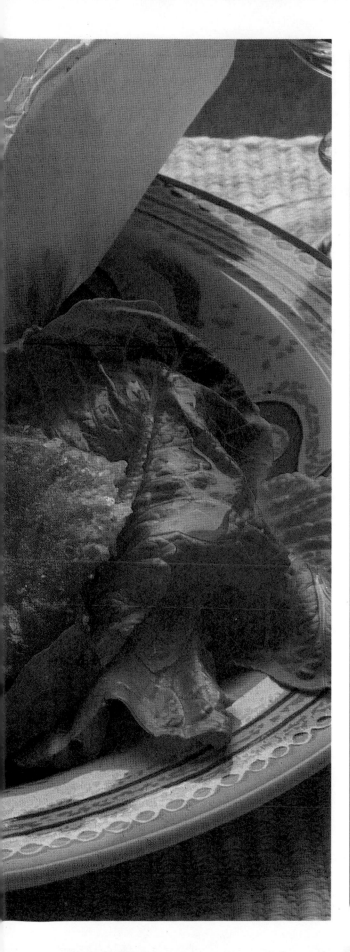

Marlene Sorosky

Menu 1
(Left)
Chicken in Parchment with Mushrooms and Tomatoes
Green Salad with Fried Goat Cheese

Marlene Sorosky's aim in the kitchen is not merely to cook an enjoyable meal. 'I specialize in beautiful food that is varied, uncomplicated, and easy to prepare,' says this California-based cooking teacher and author. Vegetables are her particular favourites, since they meet all her requirements for beautiful food. Besides, she believes that vegetables challenge home cooks to be creative; you can season and cook vegetables in an almost infinite number of ways to produce a delicious meal. There are no hard and fast rules with vegetables, she says, advising that you should simply use a common-sense approach.

Each of her three menus demonstrates her 'food-should-be-beautiful-yet-simple' philosophy. Baking and serving chicken breasts in parchment packets, as in Menu 1, is an easy but unusual way of handling a familiar dish. The recipe has an added bonus in that it leaves no pots to scrub. The vegetable-and-cheese pot pies of Menu 2 are dramatic with their golden pastry crust, yet they are easy to prepare.

In Menu 3 the spaghetti squash, topped with a red vegetable sauce, is a richly textured main course.

Boneless chicken breasts baked in parchment packets with mushrooms, tomatoes, and cheese make a perfect company meal any time of the year. To get the full impact of the vegetable aroma cut parchment packets open when you serve each person. Fried goat cheese and Romaine lettuce are an appealing side-dish combination.

Chicken in Parchment with Mushrooms and Tomatoes
Green Salad with Fried Goat Cheese

For an impressive company dinner that only *looks* complicated, serve chicken breasts with mushrooms, tomatoes, cheese, and a sauce – all assembled and wrapped in parchment packets that puff up as they cook. Kitchen parchment, which is available at speciality food shops and kitchen supply stores, preserves the natural moisture and nutrients of meats and vegetables. It also cuts down on clean-up time, a bonus. As each parchment packet heats up, some steam escapes through the porous paper, so the food does not get soggy. When you are ready to serve the chicken, snip open the packets with scissors to release a burst of aroma.

For the mushroom sauce, you use both chopped fresh mushrooms and the dried Oriental kind to intensify the mushroom flavour of the dish. Dried mushrooms, usually sold in cellophane bags, are available in well-stocked supermarkets or Oriental groceries.

For the salad with fried goat cheese, the cook recommends a log-shaped Montrachet without any black cinder coating. Chilling the crumbly cheese keeps it firm for neat and precise slicing. Freezing the slices, even briefly, helps retain their shape during the frying, which producess a crisp exterior and a soft, creamy interior.

What to drink
The presence of goat cheese in the salad justifies a red wine here: the cook suggests a Cabernet. An Alsatian Gewürztramminer or other crisp white works well also.

Start-to-Finish Steps
1 Keep goat cheese refrigerated until ready to use. Slice into eight rounds. Follow salad recipe step 1.
2 Follow chicken recipe steps 1 and 2. Chop onion, finely chop fresh mushrooms, crush garlic with flat side of chef's knife, chop parsley and basil, if using fresh basil, and core and thinly slice tomatoes. Using grater or food processor fitted with shredding disc, shred cheese.
3 Follow salad recipe steps 2 and 3.
4 Follow chicken recipe steps 3 through 7.
5 Follow salad recipe steps 4 and 5.
6 Follow chicken recipe step 8 and bring to the table with the salad.

Chicken in Parchment with Mushrooms and Tomatoes

15 g (¹/₂ oz) dried mushrooms (about 3 mushrooms), preferably Oriental
2 whole skinless, boneless chicken breasts (about 750 g (1¹/₂ lb) total weight)
2 tablespoons unsalted butter
1 onion, chopped
250 g (8 oz) fresh mushrooms, finely chopped (about 2 cups)
3 large cloves garlic, crushed
15 g (¹/₂ oz) chopped fresh parsley
1 tablespoon chopped fresh basil, or 1 teaspoon dried
Salt
Freshly ground pepper
4 tablespoons Madeira
4 tablespoons heavy cream
2 small tomatoes, cored and thinly sliced
60 g (2 oz) shredded Jarlsberg or Emmenthal cheese

1 In small bowl, soak dried mushrooms in hot water to cover for 10 minutes. Drain off liquid and reserve for another use. Rinse mushrooms and cut off and discard tough stems. Finely chop the mushrooms.
2 Trim chicken breasts of any fat and split in half.
3 In medium-size skillet, melt butter and sauté onion until soft. Add the dried and fresh mushrooms, garlic, parsley, basil, 1 teaspoon salt, and pepper to taste. Cook, stirring occasionally, until mixture is almost dry, about 7 minutes. Add Madeira and cook until evaporated, about 4 minutes. Remove pan from heat and stir in heavy cream. Season to taste.
4 Preheat oven to 240°C (475°F or Mark 9).
5 Cut 4 pieces of parchment paper into heart shapes approximately 30 cm (12 inches) long and 30 cm (12 inches) wide at top. (See diagram on next page). Unfold each heart and place 1 chicken breast half, along centrefold of each parchment heart. Sprinkle with salt and pepper.
6 Spoon an equal portion of mushroom mixture over each chicken breast half, mounding it slightly. Place 3 or 4 overlapping tomato slices over each serving and sprinkle each with 2 tablespoons of cheese.
7 Refold each heart and seal packages by starting at

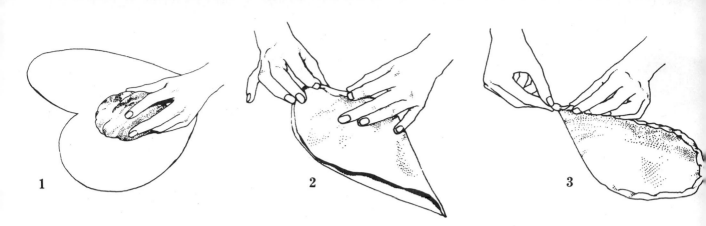

1   2   3

rounded end, rolling and crimping edges together tightly. Twist tip of heart to seal. Place packages on baking sheet, taking care not to overlap them. Bake in centre or lower third of oven 10 to 12 minutes; they should be puffed and lightly browned.

8 Remove from oven. Place on individual plates and, with scissors, cut an X in top of each package. Fold back corners and serve.

Green Salad with Fried Goat Cheese

1 egg
1 teaspoon water
30 g (1 oz) dry bread crumbs
150 g (5 oz) goat cheese, chilled and cut into 8 slices, each 5 mm-1 cm ($^1/_4$-$^1/_2$ inch) thick
1 head lettuce
2 tablespoons vegetable oil
2 tablespoons olive oil
1 teaspoon Dijon mustard
2 tablespoons red wine vinegar
Salt and freshly ground pepper
Vegetable oil for frying

1 In small bowl, beat together egg and water. Place bread crumbs on small, flat plate. Dip cheese slices in the beaten egg and coat with the bread crumbs. Place the coated slices in pie pan. Cover with foil and leave in freezer at least 30 minutes.

2 Wash lettuce and dry in salad spinner or pat dry with paper towels. Tear into bite-size pieces, wrap in kitchen towel, and refrigerate until ready to serve.

3 For salad dressing, combine vegetable oil, olive oil, mustard, vinegar, and salt and pepper to taste in large bowl or glass jar; whisk or shake until blended. Set aside.

4 In large skillet, add vegetable oil to depth of 5 mm ($^1/_4$ inch) and heat over moderate heat. Test oil by dropping in a cube of bread: if it browns lightly in 40 seconds, the oil is hot enough. Remove cheese slices from freezer and fry about 3 minutes per side, or until crisp and evenly browned. Remove to paper-towel-lined plate.

5 Remove lettuce from refrigerator, shake or whisk dressing to recombine, and toss salad with the dressing. Divide among 4 dinner or salad plates and top each serving with 2 slices of the fried goat cheese.

Deep-Dish Vegetable Pot Pies
Fresh Orange and Green Salad

When Marlene Sorosky devised this home-style, economical meal, she wanted to serve a medley of familiar vegetables in an unusual way, so she baked them in individual pot pies with puff-pastry crusts. These pies look elegant enough for company yet are wonderful for a family meal, too. All the vegetables are easy to cut up for sautéing except the onions, which you must peel. To peel them easily, the cook suggests that you first cut a small 'X' at the root end with a sharp paring knife, then place them in a pot of boiling water. Let the water return to a boil and cook the onions 3 to 5 minutes. Their skins will slip right off.

Marlene Sorosky says there are no binding rules for the vegetables you use. Be flexible and let the season guide you: choose asparagus and fresh peas in spring, courgettes and tomatoes in summer. Just use the same proportions. Although you can assemble and bake these pot pies in an hour, you can do them ahead and freeze them, unbaked, for another evening. For handling frozen puff pastry, follow package directions.

The salad of orange segments, cubed avocado, and leaf lettuce is a colourful accompaniment to the vegetable pot pie entrée. Its tart, sweet dressing provides a flavour contrast to the mildly seasoned

For an informal meal, offer vegetable pot pies with puff pastry crusts and a salad of orange sections and chopped avocado.

main course. By adding crunchy poppy seeds to the dressing, Marlene Sorosky also adds flavour and texture to the salad.

What to drink
Light young wines, either red or white, are best with this menu. The cook recommends either a California Pinot Noir or Sauvignon Blanc, but dry Chenin Blanc or Pinot Blanc are also fine choices.

Start-to-Finish Steps
1   Thaw artichoke hearts and puff pastry.
2   Rinse broccoli, trim stems, and break or cut into small florets. With paring knife, peel and slice onions. Clean mushrooms with damp paper towels and slice. If using fresh herbs, chop enough basil to measure 1 tablespoon and chop the other fresh herbs to measure 1 tablespoon. Using grater or food processor fitted with shredding disk, shred Swiss cheese and then, using metal blade, grate Parmesan.
3   Follow vegetable pies recipe steps 1 through 8.
4   About 15 minutes before vegetable pies are done, prepare salad. Peel 2 oranges, paring away the white pith, and break oranges into segments. Squeeze another orange to measure 2 tablespoons juice. Peel and mince enough onion to measure 1 tablespoon. Peel and cube avocado.
5   Follow salad steps 1 and 2, and bring to the table with the vegetable pot pies.

1   In medium-size skillet, melt 60 g (2 oz) butter. Add broccoli, onions, and mushrooms, and cook, tossing and stirring with wooden spoon, 5 minutes.
2   In large saucepan, melt remaining butter. Stir in flour and whisk over low heat 1 to 2 minutes, or until bubbling. Remove from heat and whisk in wine and half-and-half.
3   Return pan to heat and bring to a boil, whisking constantly. Stir in hot pepper sauce, salt, pepper to taste, and herbs.
4   Remove pan from heat and cool slightly. Stir in the cheeses, vegetable mixture, and artichoke hearts. Divide mixture among 4 heatproof soup bowls or casseroles.
5   Preheat oven to 200°C (400°F or Mark 6).
6   On lightly floured board, roll 1 sheet puff pastry about 5 mm (¼ inch) thick. Measure diameter of bowl; with sharp knife, cut out 4 pastry circles, each 2½-5 cm (1-2 inches) larger then the tops of the bowls.
7   In small bowl, lightly beat egg with 1 tablespoon water. With your fingers, brush rims of bowls with the egg wash. Place a pastry circle over the top of each bowl, pressing pastry over edge so that it extends at least 1½ cm (¾ inch) over sides. Press down with fork tines to seal. Brush pastry with egg wash. If desired, make decorations such as flowers or leaves with any extra pastry dough; press on top of pastry circles and brush with egg wash. You may need a second sheet of pastry dough for 4 bowls.
8   Place bowls on shallow baking sheet. Bake 20 to 25 minutes, or until pastry is puffed and browned. Let rest 10 minutes before serving.

Deep-Dish Vegetable Pot Pies

100 g (3 oz) unsalted butter
1 bunch broccoli, cut into bite-size florets
8 small white onions, peeled and sliced
250 g (8 oz) mushrooms, sliced
30 g (1 oz) plain flour
100 ml (3 fl oz) dry white wine or dry vermouth
250 ml (8 fl oz) half-and-half milk and cream
Several dashes hot pepper sauce
½ teaspoon salt
Freshly ground pepper
1 tablespoon chopped fresh basil, or 1 teaspoon dried
1 tablespoon combined chopped fresh parsley,
   chives, tarragon, and chervil, or 1 teaspoon dried
   fines herbes
175 g (6 oz) shredded Swiss cheese
60 g (2 oz) freshly grated Parmesan cheese
300 g (10 oz) frozen artichoke hearts, defrosted
250 g (8 oz) frozen puff pastry, defrosted until pliable,
   but still refrigerated
1 egg

Fresh Orange and Green Salad

1 head butter lettuce
2 small navel oranges, peeled and broken into
   segments
1 ripe avocado, peeled and cut into cubes
1 tablespoon minced onion
2 tablespoons apple cider vinegar
2 tablespoons orange juice
4 tablespoons oil, preferably peanut oil
1 teaspoon poppy seeds
¼ teaspoon dry mustard
1 teaspoon salt

1   Wash lettuce and dry in salad spinner or pat dry
    with paper towels. Tear into bite-size pieces and
    place in salad bowl. Add orange segments and
    avocado.
2   Combine onion, vinegar, orange juice, oil, poppy
    seeds, mustard, and salt in food processor or
    blender and process until well blended. Toss salad
    with just enough dressing to coat lettuce and
    orange segments. Refrigerate any remaining
    dressing to use another time.

Added touch
This dessert can be assembled ahead and baked while
you are eating the vegetable pot pies and salad. Be
sure to turn the oven temperature down to 180°C
(350°F or Mark 4) after removing the vegetable pies.

Baked Pears

4 soft ripe pears, preferably Anjou
2 tablespoons sour cream, plus additional sour
   cream for garnish (optional)
250 g (4 oz) brown sugar, firmly packed
4 tablespoons unsalted butter, at room temperature
6 tablespoons dark rum

1   Preheat oven to 180°C (350°F or Mark 4).
2   Peel, quarter, and core pears. Lay each quarter on
    its side in shallow casserole so that pears fit snugly
    in a single layer.
3   Dot pears with 2 tablespoons sour cream and
    sprinkle with brown sugar. Dot with bits of butter
    and pour rum over pears. Cover with foil and bake
    25 to 35 minutes, or until pears are barely tender
    when pierced with a fork. Serve warm, spooning
    the pan juices over the pears. Top each serving
    with additional dollop of sour cream, if desired.

Leftover suggestion
If you had a 500 g (1 lb) pack of puff pastry, you will
have 250 g (8 oz) of pastry left over from the vegetable
pies. Save it for the next time you prepare pot pies, or
use the pastry for a fruit tart. Thaw pastry, then roll
out into two 20 cm (8 inch) rounds, each 5 mm (¼
inch) thick. Cut out the centre from one of the rounds,
leaving a 2½ cm (1 inch) border. Place that border
on top of the other uncut round, and place them on
a buttered cookie sheet. Bake in a preheated 200°C
(400°F or Mark 6) oven 20 to 25 minutes, or until the
shell puffs and browns. Let cool, then fill the centre
with cut-up fresh fruit and top with whipped cream.

Spaghetti Squash with Garden Vegetable Sauce
Almond Popovers with Amaretto Butter

The cooked flesh of spaghetti squash forms long strands that look like golden-orange pasta. To cook the squash, you can boil it whole or, if you prefer, slice it in half lengthwise, set the halves cut side down in a shallow baking dish filled with 3½ cm (1½ inches) of water, and bake the halves at 190°C (375°F or Mark 5) 30 to 40 minutes, or until the flesh becomes tender. When the cooked squash is cool enough to handle, rake through the flesh with fork tines to produce the pasta-like strands. You can refrigerate the strands for later use or serve them immediately. These crunchy strands are very mildly flavoured, which makes them a perfect base for the rich vegetable-and-chicken sauce.

If you buy a squash that weighs more than two pounds, it may be difficult to cut in half unless you use a heavy cleaver. The cook suggests that you ask your produce man to halve it for you. You can refrigerate the uncooked half for later use or bake the whole squash at once and save the cooked strands for another day.

To save time, you can make the popover batter a day ahead; just stir it well before you pour it into the muffin tin or custard cups. The delicately sweet

The vegetable sauce is a colourful contrast to the pale strands of spaghetti squash. Serve popovers with almond-flavoured butter.

almond butter for the popovers calls for Amaretto, an almond-flavoured Italian liqueur. If you wish, you can eliminate both the Amaretto and the confectioners' sugar from the butter recipe and substitute 4 tablespoons honey. Crunchy almonds sprinkled on top add texture and flavour.

What to drink
The cook favours a Sauvignon Blanc with this menu, but its piquant flavours would go equally well with a simple Chianti or a California Gamay.

Start-to-Finish Steps
1 Follow spaghetti squash recipe step 1.
2 Follow almond popovers recipe steps 1 through 3. Bring butter for Amaretto butter recipe to room temperature.
3 Follow spaghetti squash recipe step 2.
4 Dice chicken, peel and cut up eggplant, and clean mushrooms with damp paper towels and slice. Chop onion, celery, green pepper, and tomatoes. Crush garlic cloves with flat side of chef's knife. Using food processor or cheese grater, grate Parmesan cheese and set aside.
5 Bake popovers, step 4.
6 Follow spaghetti squash recipe steps 3 through 5.
7 Prepare Amaretto butter, steps 1 and 2.
8 Follow spaghetti squash recipe step 6, popovers recipe step 5, and bring to the table at once with the Amaretto butter.

Spaghetti Squash with Garden Vegetable Sauce

1 medium-size spaghetti squash (about 1 Kg (2 lb)
4 tablespoons olive oil
3 boneless, skinless chicken breast halves, cut in
    1 cm (1/2 inch) dice
1 medium-size onion, chopped
1 small eggplant, peeled and cut into 1 1/2 cm (3/4 inch)
    pieces
125 g (4 oz) thickly sliced mushrooms
1 large stalk celery, coarsely chopped
60 g (2 oz) coarsely chopped green pepper
500 g (1 lb) canned whole tomatoes in thick tomato
    purée, chopped
100 g (3 oz) tomato paste
2 cloves garlic, crushed
1/2 teaspoon dried basil
1/2 teaspoon dried thyme
1/2 teaspoon dried oregano
1 bay leaf
1 teaspoon salt
Freshly ground pepper
Freshly grated Parmesan cheese

1 Bring large stockpot of water to a boil.
2 Place spaghetti squash in pot and cook 20 to 30 minutes, or until tender when pierced with a fork.
3 Meanwhile, heat olive oil in large, non-aluminium saucepan over medium heat. Add chicken, onion, and eggplant, and cook, stirring occasionally, until the onion is soft, about 10 minutes.
4 Stir in mushrooms, celery, and green pepper, and cook, stirring, until celery is barely tender, about 4 minutes.
5 Add chopped tomatoes and purée, tomato paste, garlic, and seasonings. Simmer uncovered, stirring occasionally, 20 minutes, or until sauce thickens slightly. Remove bay leaf.
6 When squash is tender, remove from pot with tongs. Cut in half lengthwise. Discard seeds and pull out squash strands with a fork. Mound squash strands on serving platter and spoon sauce over them. Sprinkle lightly with Parmesan cheese and pass additional cheese at the table, if desired.

Almond Popovers with Amaretto Butter

30 g (1 oz) whole blanched almonds
125 g (4 oz) plain flour
250 ml (8 fl oz) cup milk
2 large eggs
Dash salt
Amaretto butter (see following recipe)

1 Preheat oven to 170°C (325°F or Mark 3). Toast almonds on cookie sheet until lightly browned, about 3 to 5 minutes. Cool; sliver enough to measure 2 tablespoons and reserve 1 tablespoon for Amaretto butter garnish. Turn oven to 220°C (425°F or Mark 7).
2 In medium-size bowl, mix together flour, 1 tablespoon almonds, milk, eggs, and salt with wooden spoon until well blended. The batter may be slightly lumpy.
3 Thoroughly butter 6 custard cups, popover mold, or heavy-gauge muffin tin. Fill two thirds full with batter.
4 Bake popovers 30 to 35 minutes, or until puffed and browned.
5 Remove from oven and arrange popovers in a bread basket. Serve immediately with Amaretto butter.

Amaretto Butter

100 g (3 oz) unsalted butter, at room temperature
2 tablespoons confectioners' sugar
2 teaspoons Amaretto liqueur
¼ teaspoon almond extract
1 tablespoon toasted, blanched, slivered almonds for garnish

1   In food processor or blender, process butter and sugar or, using hand mixer, beat butter and sugar in small bowl until thoroughly blended. Slowly add Amaretto and almond extract, mixing until incorporated.
2   Turn into small serving bowl; sprinkle with slivered almonds.

Added touch

Although this dessert can be prepared quickly, it must be made far enough in advance to allow it to freeze.

Fresh Pineapple Ice

½ fresh pineapple
2 tablespoons sugar
1 tablespoon lemon juice
2 tablespoons kirsch

1   Halve, core, and peel pineapple half. Cut into 2½ cm (1 inch) chunks and purée in 2 batches in food processor or blender. There should be about 350 g (12 oz) of purée. (If you have less, reduce sugar to taste.)
2   Stir in 125 ml (4 fl oz) of water, sugar, lemon juice, and kirsch. Spoon the purée into divided ice cube trays. Freeze until solid, at least 2 hours.
3   Before serving, process 4 to 6 of the pineapple cubes at a time in food processor or blender. Turn machine on and off until cubes are broken up. Process until mixture becomes a velvety slush.
4   Spoon into bowls and serve immediately.

Peeling and Slicing a Pineapple

1 Removing the top. With a sharp, stainless steel knife (here, a medium-sized chef's knife), slice off the pineapple's bushy green top. Turn the fruit round and slice off 2.5 cm (1 inch) or so from the bottom.

2 Removing the skin. Stand the pineapple on end and slice off a strip of skin, following the contour of the fruit. Cut deep enough to remove most of the dark eyes. Continue slicing until all the skin is removed.

3 Cutting slices. Cut out any of the eyes that remain. Place the fruit on its side and, steadying it with one hand, divide the pineapple into as many slices as the recipe calls for.

4 Coring the slices. With a small biscuit cutter, as shown here, or an apple corer, firmly stamp out and discard the tough, fibrous centre of each pineapple slice. If you do not have a small cutter or a corer, remove the centre with the tip of a paring knife.

Beverly Cox

Menu 1
(*Right*)
Eggplant Pie
Green Bean and Onion Salad
Oranges with Cinnamon

To Beverly Cox, a perfectly cooked meal must be nutritionally balanced as well as delicious and artistic. She adapts her classic French training to a lighter style of cooking that focuses on garden-fresh produce. She experiments with converting vegetable side dishes into complete main courses, often turning to the Cajun cooking of Louisiana for ideas.

Because she likes vegetables slightly undercooked, Beverly Cox relies on two methods for cooking them: steaming and quick-boiling. Steaming preserves the nutrients, colours, and crunchy textures of vegetables, as well as prevents them from becoming waterlogged. On the other hand, quick-boiling has its advantages, too. It tenderizes vegetables and diminishes the tart or bitter taste of some. After you remove the vegetables from the boiling water, 'refresh' them – that is, dunk them into cold water, which stops the cooking and sets the colour.

The entrées in the first two menus are substantial vegetable dishes. The eggplant pie of Menu 1 is a good example of a vegetable main course that can stand on its own nutritionally. In menu 2, mirlitons, green pear-shaped squash, are stuffed with shrimp, ham, and seasonings for a satisfying Louisiana-style dish. Beverly Cox seasons the stuffing with Cajun red-pepper sauce.

Even though the entrée in Menu 3 cooks at once in one pot, it is not a stew. This energy-efficient cooking method is a legacy from Oriental Kitchens, where cooks often steam and lightly poach their foods. A particular bonus is that there is only one pot to clean.

This substantial menu, ideal for a company lunch, is rich with colour and texture. Sprinkle the baked eggplant pie with grated Parmesan cheese just before you serve it, if you wish. Pass the bundles of green beans, held by red pepper rings, on a serving dish or on chilled salad plates. Orange sections with cinnamon come to the table in a serving bowl.

Menu 1

Eggplant Pie
Green Bean and Onion Salad
Oranges with Cinnamon

This main-course eggplant pie resembles a quiche, but it is baked without a pastry crust; instead, Beverly Cox forms the crust from unpeeled eggplant slices to hold the cheese-egg-vegetable filling. When shopping, select eggplants that feel heavy and have smooth, flawless, shiny purple skins. Brown rough spots indicate probable decay or improper handling. Refrigerated, eggplant can keep up to six weeks. Because eggplant that is not perfectly ripe can taste bitter, Beverly Cox calls for parboiling the slices for several minutes to render any bitter juices. You can peel or not peel the eggplant as you wish: remember that the skin adds some flavour and also helps keep the slices intact.

The dessert – orange slices sparked with ground cinnamon – is a Moroccan combination. To make this fruit salad, select seedless oranges. When you peel them, remove as much bitter white pith as possible. Use a sharp paring knife to peel the skin off in a spiral, following the contours of the fruit.

What to drink

The brightness of the flavors in this menu call for a fresh and fruity red wine, such as an Italian Dolcetto or a Californian Gamay.

Start-to-Finish Steps

1 Follow eggplant pie recipe step 1. While water comes to a boil, peel and halve garlic, mince enough onion to measure 3 tablespoons, and mince enough parsley to measure 1 tablespoon. If using canned tomatoes, peel, if necessary, and seed and chop them. If using fresh tomatoes, blanch them 30 seconds in small saucepan of boiling water. Then peel, seed, and chop.
2 Follow eggplant pie recipe steps 2 through 7.
3 While sauce is cooking, follow salad recipe steps 1 through 5, using large saucepan just used for parboiling eggplant.
4 Slice mozzarella and tomato, and follow eggplant pie recipe steps 8 through 13.
5 Follow salad recipe steps 6 through 8.
6 Prepare oranges recipe, steps 1 through 5.
7 Grate cheese and follow eggplant pie recipe step 14.
8 Follow salad recipe step 9.
9 Follow eggplant pie recipe step 15 and serve with green bean salad. Serve oranges with cinnamon for dessert.

Eggplant Pie

1 medium-size eggplant (approximately 250 g (8 oz))
1 clove garlic, peeled and halved
3 tablespoons olive oil
Salt
Freshly ground pepper
3 tablespoons minced onion
350 g (12 oz) peeled, seeded, and chopped tomatoes, canned or fresh (about 4 whole tomatoes)
1 tablespoon minced fresh parsley
1/4 teaspoon dried oregano
1/4 teaspoon dried basil
250 g (8 oz) thinly sliced mozzarella
6 tomato slices (about 1 large tomato)
2 whole eggs
1 teaspoon capers
2 egg whites
1 tablespoon freshly grated Romano cheese

1 In large covered saucepan, bring 1 ltr (2 pts) of water to a boil.
2 Preheat oven to 190°C (375°F or Mark 5).
3 Rinse eggplant and slice into 1 cm (1/2 inch) rounds. Parboil slices 3 minutes, drain in colander, and pat dry, squeezing out excess moisture with paper towels.
4 Rub inside of 25 cm (10 inch) pie plate with halved clove of garlic; discard garlic. Pour in 2 tablespoons of the olive oil. Coat both sides of the eggplant slices with the oil and arrange them in pie plate so that they cover bottom and extend partway up sides. Sprinkle lightly with salt and pepper.
5 Place pie plate on middle rack in oven while you prepare the tomato mixture.
6 In large skillet, heat remaining 1 tablespoon olive oil. Add onion and sauté until onion is transparent and soft.
7 Add chopped tomatoes, parsley, oregano, basil, and salt and pepper to taste. Cook over medium heat, stirring often, until sauce cooks down and thickens slightly, about 10 minutes.
8 After sauce has thickened, remove eggplant from oven. Cover eggplant with mozzarella slices and top with tomato slices.
9 Crack whole eggs into medium-size mixing bowl. Whisk until light and frothy.

10 Stir tomato mixture into the eggs. Add capers and salt and pepper to taste.

11 Using electric hand mixer, beat egg whites with pinch of salt in separate bowl until they form soft peaks.

12 Gently fold the egg whites into the tomato-egg mixture until thoroughly incorporated.

13 Pour mixture into pie plate and bake on rack in middle of oven 20 minutes.

14 Sprinkle with grated cheese and return to oven for 5 to 10 minutes more, or until eggs are thoroughly set and top is lightly browned.

15 Remove pie from oven; cool a few minutes. Cut pie into wedges and serve.

Green Bean and Onion Salad

500 g (1 lb) green beans
1 large red bell pepper
3 small or 2 large scallions
1 large lemon
2 teaspoons red wine vinegar
2 teaspoons Dijon mustard
125 ml (4 fl oz) olive oil
Salt and freshly ground pepper
4 lettuce leaves for garnish (optional)

1 In saucepan fitted with collapsible vegetable steamer, bring $2^{1}/_{2}$ cm (1 inch) of water to a boil.

2 Rinse beans, pepper, and scallions under cold running water.

3 Remove strings from beans and trim ends. Steam beans, covered, until just tender, about 3 to 4 minutes.

4 While beans are cooking, wash pepper; core and seed through stem end, leaving shell intact. Cut pepper shell into thin rings; set aside.

5 Place beans in colander and refresh them under cold running water.

6 Slice scallions into thin rings. Squeeze lemon to measure $3^{1}/_{2}$ teaspoons juice. Reserve $1^{1}/_{2}$ teaspoons for oranges recipe.

7 In small mixing bowl, combine 2 teaspoons lemon juice, wine vinegar, and mustard. Add olive oil in a slow, steady stream, whisking constantly.

8 Place the well-drained beans in flat serving bowl and toss with the dressing and scallions. Sprinkle with salt and pepper to taste. Marinate 15 minutes before serving.

9 When ready to assemble, group the beans in small bundles. Slip a red pepper ring around the centre of each bundle. To serve, place the bundles on chilled serving plátter, lined with lettuce leaves, if desired. Sprinkle scallions and any dressing remaining in the bowl over the bundles.

Oranges with Cinnamon

4 oranges
$1^{1}/_{2}$ teaspoons lemon juice
Cinnamon
Honey or sugar (optional)

1 Peel oranges, removing all the white inner skin.

2 Holding a peeled orange over a serving bowl to catch the juice, cut with sharp paring knife between section membranes and let sections fall into bowl.

3 Squeeze remaining membranes to remove any juice. Discard membranes. Repeat with remaining oranges.

4 Add reserved lemon juice to the orange sections and sprinkle with cinnamon to taste.

5 Check for sweetness and add honey or sugar to taste, if desired. Cover and refrigerate until ready to serve for dessert.

Louisiana-Style Mirlitons Stuffed with Ham and Shrimp
Marinated Carrots

Arrange this Southern-style meal of ham-and-shrimp-stuffed mirlitons and marinated carrot slices on individual dinner plates. Garnish the carrots with chopped parsley or sliced scallions, or both.

In the USA, Southern cooks often use a pear-shaped winter squash called mirliton, also known as chayote squash in the West Indies, Mexico, and the Southwest. This green squash tastes somewhat like a cucumber and is a good flavour contrast for savoury fillings. Many supermarkets and greengrocers nationwide now stock mirlitons. If you cannot find them, you can use green bell peppers. If so, parboil the peppers before you stuff and bake them. Or, you can substitute any winter squash (except spaghetti squash). The taste will differ, but the textures will be similar. When you shop for this meal, select mirlitons that are dark green and firm. You can store them for up to two weeks in the refrigerator.

The ham-and-shrimp stuffing, seasoned with onion, garlic, herbs, and hot-pepper sauce, is Louisiana style: ham and shrimp are ubiquitous ingredients there, as is the piquant pepper sauce.

The carrots, which Beverly Cox often has enjoyed in the South, make an unusual salad or side dish. It is important that you select firm carrots of uniform size for the fullest flavour and the most attractive slices. After peeling the carrots, cut them on the bias into 2¹/₂ cm (1 inch) thick pieces and steam them until just tender. The steaming makes them porous enough to absorb some of the vinaigrette. Serve the salad at room temperature for maximum flavor.

What to drink
The harmony of ingredients here demands a medium-bodied, not-too-obtrusive white wine, such as an Entre-Deux-Mers or a young white Bordeaux.

Start-to-Finish Steps
1 Follow mirlitons recipe steps 1.
2 For mirlitons recipe, rinse shrimp in colander. Using sharp paring knife or small pair of scissors, peel and devein shrimp. Dice shrimp and ham, peel and finely chop onion, peel and mince garlic clove, mince enough parsley to measure 1 tablespoon, and, if using fresh thyme, mince a few sprigs to measure ¹/₄ teaspoon. Process enough bread in food processor or blender to make bread crumbs. Lightly grease baking sheet.
3 Follow mirlitons recipe steps 3 through 8.
4 While the mirlitons are baking, follow marinated carrots recipe steps 1 through 5, using steamer used for mirlitons.

5 Follow mirlitons recipe step 9 and marinated carrots recipe step 6, and bring to the table.

Louisiana-Style Mirlitons Stuffed with Ham and Shrimp

4 small or 2 large mirlitons (chayote squash)
3 tablespoons unsalted butter
350 g (12 oz) fresh shrimp, peeled, deveined, and finely diced
250 g (8 oz) cooked ham, finely diced
100 g (3 oz) finely chopped onion
1 large clove garlic, minced
$^1/_4$ teaspoon hot pepper sauce
1 tablespoon minced fresh parsley
$^1/_4$ teaspoon minced fresh thyme, or pinch dried thyme
Salt
Freshly ground black pepper
100 g (3 oz) unseasoned fresh bread crumbs, preferably freshly made from day-old French or white bread
Vegetable oil or butter for greasing baking sheet

1 In large covered saucepan fitted with collapsible vegetable steamer, bring 2$^1/_2$ cm (1 inch) of water to a boil.
2 Cut squash in half and remove seeds. Steam halves, cut side down, 30 to 35 minutes, or until they are tender but still hold their shape. Check water level occasionally, adding more water if necessary.
3 While mirlitons are steaming, melt 2 tablespoons of the butter in large skillet. Add shrimp, ham, onion, garlic, and hot pepper sauce, and cook over medium heat, stirring often with a wooden spoon, until onions become transparent.
4 Preheat oven to 190°C (375°F or Mark 5).
5 Using tongs, remove squash and drain on paper towels. Carefully scoop out pulp into medium-size bowl, leaving 1 cm ($^1/_2$ inch) thick shells. Place shells on lightly greased baking sheet.
6 To the skillet, add mashed mirliton pulp, parsley, thyme, and salt and pepper to taste. Cook another 5 minutes, then stir in all but 2 tablespoons of the bread crumbs and mix well.
7 Fill mirliton shells with the cooked mixture. Sprinkle with remaining bread crumbs and dot with remaining tablespoon butter.
8 Bake in upper third of oven 10 to 15 minutes, or until tops are lightly browned.
9 Remove from oven and, with wide metal spatula, place the stuffed mirlitons on individual serving plates. Serve at once.

Marinated Carrots

500 g (1 lb) carrots
2 tablespoons finely sliced scallions, both green and white parts
2 tablespoons minced fresh parsley
$^1/_4$ teaspoon oregano
Salt and freshly ground pepper
5 tablespoons olive oil
2 tablespoons red wine vinegar
Parsley sprigs for garnish (optional)

1 In large covered saucepan fitted with collapsible vegetable steamer, bring 2$^1/_2$ cm (1 inch) of water to a boil.
2 Peel carrots and cut on diagonal into pieces 2$^1/_2$ cm (1 inch) long and 1 cm ($^1/_2$ inch) wide. Steam 2 minutes, or until barely tender. Drain carrots in colander and turn into serving dish.
3 Trim and slice scallions, and mince parsley. Sprinkle carrots with scallions, parsley, oregano, and salt and pepper to taste.
4 Pour olive oil and vinegar over carrots. Toss lightly.
5 Allow carrots to marinate at least 15 minutes at room temperature before serving.
6 Serve carrots in the marinade and garnish with parsley sprigs, if desired.

Menu 3

Chicken Breasts with a Bouquet of Vegetables and Sweet-and-Sour Sauce
Green Salad with Herbed Vinaigrette

The cooking method for the chicken-and-vegetables entrée may seem complicated at first, yet it is systematic and an excellent technique to add to your repertoire. Using a large vegetable steamer with a wire basket, or a large covered saucepan with a colander, poach the leeks, cabbage leaves, garlic, and chicken breasts in apple cider. Simultaneously, steam the carrot slices, then the courgette slices, in the basket or colander above the liquid, which you then cook down and use as the base for the sweet-and-sour sauce. Lightly steamed carrots and courgettes retain their natural flavour and crunch. Because you add the ingredients in stages, nothing overcooks.

Beverly Cox calls for unsweetened apple cider, preferably filtered for a more translucent sauce. Avoid using a sweetened cider or a standard apple juice, both of which would produce an overly sweet sauce. If apple juice is your only option, choose one made from tart apples, such as McIntosh. After removing the chicken and vegetables from the liquid, add a good-quality, red wine vinegar and Dijon mustard, and cook until the seasoned cider thickens and becomes translucent.

Red cabbage leaves from individual 'baskets' for the chicken and assorted vegetables. Serve the tart-sweet sauce for the main course in a pitcher or sauce boat, and the tossed green salad on separate plates.

The greens for the salad are lettuce and slightly tart escarole. To select the greens, look for full, round heads of lettuce with crisp, unwilted leaves. Before refrigerating, rinse the lettuce well in cold water, taking care not to bruise the leaves. Drain them well, and pat them as dry as possible. Wrap them in a clean dish towel and store in the refrigerator until dinner time. Escarole, a variety of endive available all year, is a bushy green with broad leaves. Select and handle escarole just as you would lettuce.

What to drink

To accompany this medley of sweet and sharp tastes, you need a wine with its own concert of sweet and dry elements. A good Moselle of the Kabinett or Spatlese class would do very well, but perhaps the best complement to the main dish would be a good Washington State Riesling, which has a characteristic delicate apple aroma.

Start-to-Finish Steps

1 Mince mint and garlic, snip chives, and follow green salad recipe step 1.
2 Follow chicken breasts recipe steps 1 through 4.
3 Follow green salad recipe step 2.
4 Clean salad greens, step 3.
5 Preheat oven to 200 degrees. Follow chicken breasts recipe steps 5 through 9.
6 Follow green salad recipe step 4, chicken breasts recipe step 10, and serve.

Chicken Breasts with a Bouquet of vegetables and Sweet-and-sour Sauce

1½ ltrs (3 pts) unsweetened apple cider
3 leeks
Small head red cabbage
2 garlic cloves
2 whole skinless, boneless chicken breasts, halved
    (about 750 g (1½ lb) total weight)
6 medium-size carrots
3 medium-size courgettes
1½ tablespoons red wine vinegar
1½ tablespoons Dijon mustard
Fresh parsley sprigs for garnish (optional)

1 Pour cider into bottom of large steamer unit or covered saucepan large enough to hold a colander. Bring to a boil.

2 Trim off root ends of leeks. Split lengthwise, gently spread leaves, and rinse well to remove any sand and grit. Cut each leek crosswise into 5 mm (¼ inch) slices. Trim cabbage of limp or darkened outer leaves, rinse, and remove 16 small leaves. Peel garlic.

3 Add leeks, cabbage leaves, and whole garlic to the cider. Reduce heat to a simmer and cook 5 minutes.

4 Halve chicken breasts, add to cider mixture, and return cider to a boil. Cover, reduce heat, and simmer 10 minutes.

5 Meanwhile, peel and trim carrots. Cut them into 5 cm (2 inch) lengths and cut each piece lengthwise into quarters. Place steamer basket or colander in pan. Add carrots, cover, and steam 3 minutes.

6 Wash and trim courgettes. Cut on diagonal into 1 cm (½ inch) ovals. Add to steamer basket and

steam, covered, another 3 minutes. The vegetables should remain crisp.

7 Remove steamer basket or colander and with slotted spoon remove remaining vegetables and chicken from the poaching liquid. Discard garlic. Arrange cabbage, carrots, courgettes, and leeks in a decorative border on each dinner plate. Place 1 chicken breast half in centre of each plate. Keep warm in oven.

8 Bring liquid to a boil, uncovered, and cook until reduced to one third the original amount, about 5 to 10 minutes. You should have about 500 ml (1 pt).

9 Whisk vinegar and mustard into the reduced liquid and cook until it becomes syrupy and translucent, about 5 to 7 minutes.

10 Remove plates from oven. Spoon sauce over the chicken. Garnish with parsley, if desired, and serve at once.

Green Salad with Herbed Vinaigrette

1 tablespoon minced fresh mint
1½ teaspoons snipped chives, preferably fresh
½ teaspoons minced garlic
6 tablespoons peanut or safflower oil
2 tablespoons red wine vinegar
Salt and freshly ground pepper
2 heads lettuce
Small head escarole

1 In small bowl, marinate mint, chives, and garlic in oil 15 to 20 minutes

2 Pour vinegar into another small bowl and gradually whisk in the oil and herbs. Season with salt and pepper to taste. Set aside.

3 Trim salad greens of any limp or browned outer leaves, root ends, and core. Wash well and dry in salad spinner or drain in colander and pat dry with paper towels. Wrap in kitchen towel and refrigerate until ready to use.

4 Just before serving, place greens in salad bowl and toss with vinaigrette.

Rinse leeks thoroughly to remove sand and grit.

Added touch

The surprise ingredient in this delicious cake is puréed beetroot. It not only tints the batter, but it adds moisture as well.

Spicy Chocolate Beet Cake

1½ Kg (3 lb) cooked beetroot
6 eggs
625 g (1¼ lb) granulated sugar
100 g (3 oz) dark brown sugar
350 ml (12 fl oz) vegetable oil
450 g (14 oz) sifted plain flour
4 teaspoons baking soda
½ teaspoon salt
¼ teaspoon ground cloves
¼ teaspoon cinnamon
5 ounces unsweetened baking chocolate
1¼ teaspoons vanilla extract
Chocolate glaze (see following recipe)

1 Preheat oven to 180°C (350°F or Mark 4).
2 Butter and flour 25 cm (10 inch) angel food cake pan or Bundt pan.
3 Drain beetroot well and purée it in food processor or blender. Set aside.
4 In large mixing bowl, beat eggs with hand mixer until pale yellow and frothy. Gradually beat in both the sugars and the oil, combining well.
5 Using spatula, fold beetroot purée into egg mixture.
6 Sift flour onto a sheet of waxed paper, then sift baking soda, salt, cloves, and cinnamon into the flour and mix together well. Gradually fold dry ingredients into the beetroot mixture, making sure to combine well.
7 Melt chocolate in top of double boiler over simmering water. With spatula, fold chocolate and vanilla extract into the cake batter, continuing to mix gently until thoroughly incorporated.
8 Pour batter into prepared cake pan and bake in middle of oven 1½ hours, or until cake is firm to the touch and a toothpick or straw comes out clean when inserted in centre of cake.
9 Invert cake onto baking rack and cool *completely* before frosting with chocolate glaze.

Chocolate Glaze

175 g (6 oz) semisweet baking chocolate
1 tablespoon unsalted butter
1 tablespoon light corn syrup
175 ml (6 fl oz) heavy cream
Pinch of salt
½ teaspoon vanilla extract
Dash of cinnamon (optional)

1 Melt chocolate in top of double boiler.
2 Stir in butter and corn syrup, then gradually mix in cream. Continue to stir over simmering water until mixture is smooth and well blended, about 1 minute. Add salt, vanilla, and cinnamon, and stir again.
3 Set the thoroughly cooled cake still on its rack over a pan to catch any drippings and pour or drip the warm glaze over top of cake.
4 Lift rack and gently shake it to distribute the glaze evenly. Chill cake until glaze is set, about 20 to 30 minutes.

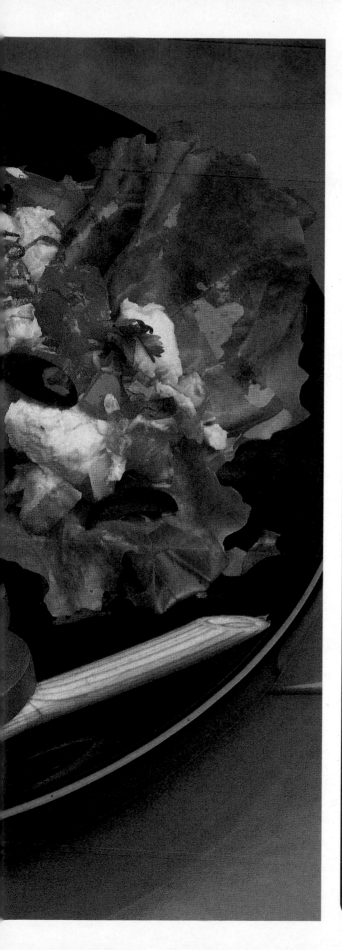

Jane Salzfass Freiman

Menu 1
(*Left*)
Seafood Salad
Cheese and Scallion Enchiladas
with Guacamole

Because she grew up in California, where fruits and vegetables grow in abundance year round, Jane Salzfass Freiman says that fresh produce is integral to her menu planning. Now living in Chicago, she picks her own vegetables from her garden during the growing season, and, throughout the year, she serves at least one, sometimes two, fresh vegetable dishes each day – either a vegetable appetizer, often an Italian-style recipe, or a vegetable entrée and a salad, both in the same meal.

Through her cooking class and syndicated food column, Jane Salzfass Freiman promotes the use of fresh, natural ingredients of all kinds. Moreover, she creates recipes that stress strong, direct flavours, as in all three of the meals here. Menu 1 features two piquant Mexican-style courses, a seafood salad that is a modified version of *seviche*, in which fish requires overnight 'cooking' in the acid of citrus-fruit juice. Her version speeds up the original recipe by quick-poaching the seafood and then marinating it in lime and orange juices. The accompanying enchiladas are covered with a guacamole spiked with jalapeño chilies. Both the watercress soup and the red-pepper sauce for the grilled cod of Menu 2 have assertive flavours that nonetheless balance each other. In menu 3, she brings together a mildly seasoned pasta entrée with the fresh, powerful flavours of fennel and radicchio.

This Mexican-style meal features cheese-and-scallion-stuffed enchiladas and a chilled marinated seafood salad. When you serve the enchiladas, top each with a portion of the guacamole sauce and then with a spoonful of sour cream and a sliver of tomato. Sliced black olives and chopped coriander add colour to the seafood salad.

Seafood Salad
Cheese and Scallion Enchiladas with Guacamole Sauce

This casual meal requires several Mexican ingredients, one of them corn tortillas for the main dish. Fresh corn tortillas, sealed in plastic bags, may be found in the dairy section of most supermarkets. If you buy paper-wrapped, fresh tortillas, remember that they dry out quickly, so store them in a tightly sealed plastic bag.

This guacamole sauce contains several unusual seasonings. Tomatillos – tart, green, and available year round – resemble tiny tomatoes. Fresh tomatillos have a paper-like skin that you peel away before cooking. Tomatillos are available at some supermarkets. Select those that are yellow-green and do not have any bruises or discolourations. Canned tomatillos are on the gourmet shelves of well-stocked supermarkets and are acceptable substitutes. Coriander, also known as cilantro, or Chinese parsley, has a distinctve, earthy taste intrinsic to many Mexican and Oriental recipes. It has flat, pale-green leaves like Italian parsley; treat coriander as you would regular parsley. Fresh jalapeño peppers are readily available in many parts of the country, but you will find canned or pickled jalapeños at any supermarket that stocks Mexican ingredients. Handle jalapeño peppers with care. If possible, wear thin rubber gloves when you touch them; if you do handle them with your bare hands, be sure not to touch your eyes or mouth until you have washed your hands thoroughly with soap and water.

What to drink
To accompany these dishes, choose a crisp, fruity, dry white wine, such as an Italian Soave or Verdicchio, a California Chenin Blanc, or a French Vouvray.

Start-to-Finish Steps
At least 30 minutes ahead: If using frozen tortillas for enchiladas, remove from the freezer and unwrap.

1. Follow guacamole recipe step 1.
2. Lightly rinse and pat dry cod and scallops for seafood salad and follow recipe steps 1 through 3, using same saucepan used for cooking tomatillos.
3. Squeeze juices for seafood salad and for guacamole. Follow seafood salad recipe steps 4 and 5.
4. Prepare tortillas for enchiladas, steps 1 and 2.
5. Follow seafood salad recipe step 6.

6. Follow enchiladas recipe steps 3 through 6. Sliver tomato for garnish.
7. While enchiladas are baking, peel garlic, trim scallion, and dice jalapeño peppers for guacamole sauce. Follow steps 2 through 4.
8. Sliver olives and slice lime, if using for garnish, and complete seafood salad recipe, steps 7 and 8.
9. When enchiladas are baked, follow recipe step 7, and serve with the seafood salad.

Seafood Salad

Small bunch coriander
125 g (4 oz) shrimp, unshelled
125 g (4 oz) fresh cod fillet
125 g (4 oz) bay scallops, or sea scallops, cut into 5 mm (1/4 inch) dice
1/2 medium onion
1 large ripe tomato
4 tablespoons fresh lime juice
100 ml (3 fl oz) fresh orange juice
1/4 teaspoon salt
Pinch of sugar
Several dashes of hot pepper sauce
Small head lettuce
Black olives, slivered, for garnish (optional)

1. Immerse coriander in bowl of cold water to soak.
2. In covered medium-sized saucepan, bring 500 ml (1 pt) of water to a rolling boil. Add shrimp and cook briefly, about 2 minutes, or until they turn pink. Using slotted spoon, transfer shrimp to colander and refresh under cold running water. Add fish and scallops to the boiling water. Turn off heat, cover, and set aside 5 minutes.
3. Shell and devein shrimp. Cut into 5 mm (1/4 inch) dice. Place in flat, glass baking dish.
4. Peel and cut onion into 2 1/2 mm (1/8 inch) dice; set aside. Core and cut tomato into 5 mm (1/4 inch) dice; Add onion, tomato, lime juice, orange juice, salt, sugar, and hot pepper sauce to baking dish, and stir to combine. Refrigerate mixture.
5. Using slotted spoon, remove fish and scallops from pan, and drain in colander. Carefully check fish and discard any stray bones. With fork, separate fish fillet into flakes. While fish and

36

scallops are still hot, add to dish in refrigerator and stir to combine.

6 Drain coriander and remove stems. Dry in salad spinner or pat dry with paper towels. Reserve 15 g (¹/₂ oz) firmly packed coriander for guacamole sauce. Wrap remainder in towel; refrigerate until ready to use.

7 Just before serving, mince 2 tablespoons of coriander and add to fish. Stir to combine; taste for seasoning.

8 Serve seafood salad on lettuce leaves, garnished with slivers of black olives, if desired.

Cheese and Scallion Enchiladas

8 corn tortillas, each about 6 inches in diameter
2 scallions
250 g (8 oz) mature cheddar cheese, chilled
3 tablespoons unsalted butter
Guacamole sauce (see following recipe)
4 heaped tablespoonfuls sour cream
1 small ripe tomato, slivered, for garnish

1 Adjust oven rack to middle position. Preheat oven to 220°C (425°F or Mark 7).

2 Stack tortillas and wrap in foil. Heat in oven until warm and flexible, about 6 to 8 minutes.

3 Trim scallions and slice into thin rings.

4 Using food processor or cheese grater, shred cheese.

5 In small saucepan, melt butter. Using pastry brush, brush rectangular baking dish with melted butter. Brush 1 side of each tortilla with melted butter, reserving a tablespoonful. Divide cheese evenly down centre of tortillas, then sprinkle with scallions. Tightly roll tortillas and place them side by side in baking dish, folded side down. Gently press tortillas to help keep them from unfolding. Brush tops of tortillas with remaining butter and cover dish tightly with foil.

6 Bake 12 to 15 minutes, or until cheese melts. Remove from oven and loosen foil to allow steam to escape.

7 Using wide, metal spatula, place 2 enchiladas on each dinner plate. Cover each enchilada generously with guacamole sauce and garnish each with a heaped spoonful of sour cream and a tomato sliver. Serve immediately.

Guacamole Sauce

7 fresh tomatillos (about 250 g (8 oz)) or 350 g (12 oz) canned
2 medium-size cloves garlic, peeled
1 scallion, trimmed
15 g (¹/₂ oz) firmly packed fresh coriander
1¹/₂ teaspoons to 1 tablespoon diced, canned jalapeño peppers, according to taste
1 large avocado (about 350 g (12 oz))
1 tablespoon fresh lemon juice
1 tablespoon vegetable oil
³/₄ teaspoon salt (approximately)

1 If using fresh tomatillos, remove and discard paper-like skins; rinse tomatillos. Place tomatillos in medium-size saucepan with cold water to cover. Cover pan, bring water to a boil, and cook 1 minute. Drain in colander, then place tomatillos in bowl of ice water. Set aside. If using canned tomatillos, simply drain in strainer, rinse, and set aside. (They are already cooked.)

2 Chop garlic, scallion, and coriander in food processor or blender. Add jalapeños and process until ingredients are minced. If using fresh tomatillos, first drain them in strainer. Then halve tomatillos and add them to processor. Process until puréed and well combined, scraping down sides of container with rubber spatula as necessary.

3 Halve avocado and remove pit. Peel and slice avocado, add to mixture, and process to combine well.

4 Add lemon juice, oil, and salt to taste. Process once more. Set sauce aside at room temperature until ready to serve enchiladas. Just before serving, taste again and adjust seasonings if necessary.

Watercress Soup
Grilled Cod with Red-Pepper Sauce
Steamed New Potatoes

The colourful garnishes here will enhance this meal of watercress soup, cod with red-pepper sauce, and new potatoes.

What to drink

The cook recommends a California Fumé Blanc or an Italian Pinot Grigio for this meal. A light red wine, such as a very young Zinfandel, is another possibility.

Start-to-Finish Steps

1 Trim root ends and leafy green tops from scallions. Cut each scallion into lengths. Peel baking potato and cube. Follow watercress soup recipe steps 1 through 3.

2 Peel and slice shallot; rinse, core, seed, and cut red bell pepper into squares; and with tweezers remove small bones from fillets. Follow broiled cod recipe steps 1 and 2.

3 Scrub new potatoes and follow recipe steps 1 and 2.

4 Follow soup recipe steps 4 through 7.

5 Follow cod recipe steps 3 through 5.

6 Follow watercress soup recipe step 8 and serve

7 Follow cod recipe steps 6 through 8 and potatoes recipe step 3. Serve at once.

Watercress Soup

4 scallions, trimmed and cut into 2¹/₂ cm (1 inch)
   lengths
1 baking potato (about 250 g (8 oz)), peeled and
   cubed
750 ml (1¹/₂ pts) chicken stock
125 ml (4 fl oz) milk
1 to 2 bunches watercress (about 175 g (6 oz))
¹/₄ teaspoon salt
Twist of freshly ground white pepper
Several dashes hot pepper sauce
125 ml (4 fl oz) heavy cream

1 In food processor fitted with metal blade or in
   blender, chop scallions. With machine running,
   add potato cubes, and then in a slow, steady
   stream add ¹/₃ of the chicken stock. Process until
   potato is puréed.
2 Transfer purée to large, heavy-guage non-stick
   aluminium saucepan. With slotted spoon, stir in
   remaining stock and milk. Cover and simmer
   about 15 minutes.
3 Wash watercress, discard stems, and drain leaves.
   Dry in salad spinner or pat dry with paper towels.
4 Put watercress, salt, pepper, and hot pepper sauce
   in processor bowl or blender (there is no need to
   wash it). Process until watercress is finely minced,
   scraping down sides of container with rubber
   spatula.
5 Bring purée-stock mixture to a simmer. Add half
   the cream in a slow, steady stream, stirring to
   combine.
6 Return liquid to a simmer. Add half the liquid to the
   watercress. Process about 1 minute. Empty into
   large mixing bowl. Add remaining liquid to
   processor. Process 30 seconds and add to mixture
   in bowl and stir to blend.
7 Wipe out saucepan with paper towels and return
   all the soup to it. Adjust seasonings to taste and
   keep covered until ready to serve.
8 Before serving, reheat soup, stirring occasionally,
   over low heat. Do not allow soup to boil. To serve,
   garnish each portion with a tablespoon of the
   remaining cream.

Grilled Cod with Red-Pepper Sauce

350 ml (12 fl oz) dry white wine
1 medium-size shallot, peeled and sliced
1 large red bell pepper
500-750 g (1-1¹/₂ lb) skinless cod fillets, bones
   removed
2 tablespoons olive or vegetable oil
Salt
1 tablespoon white wine vinegar
150 g (5 oz) unsalted butter
Freshly ground white pepper

1 In medium-size saucepan, combine white wine,
   shallot, and red pepper. Boil uncovered over high
   heat until no more than 2 tablespoons of liquid
   remain in pan, about 10 minutes. Remove from
   heat and set aside to cool slightly.
2 Rinse fish fillets and pat dry. Cut into 4 equal
   portions. Rub both sides with oil, and sprinkle
   lightly with salt.
3 Process red pepper and liquid in food processor or
   blender until smooth. Return mixture to saucepan.
   Using wooden spoon, stir in vinegar and about
   ¹/₄ teaspoon salt. Add ²/₃ of the butter, cut into
   pieces, whisking continuously over low heat until
   butter melts, about 5 minutes.
4 Place grill rack 10 cm (4 inches) from heat source
   and preheat grill pan.
5 Strain sauce over medium-size bowl, using a
   spoon to push it through mesh. Wipe the saucepan
   clean, pour strained sauce into it, and set aside.
6 Place cod on hot grill pan and grill 5 to 6 minutes,
   or until fish is opaque.
7 Meanwhile, turn heat to low under pepper sauce.
   Whisk in remaining butter, in pieces. Taste; add
   salt and white pepper to taste. When sauce is
   heated through, spoon about 4 tablespoonfuls
   onto each dinner plate.
8 When fish is done, remove immediately from grill
   pan with wide, metal spatula. Place fish on sauce.

Steamed New Potatoes

500 g (1 lb) small, new potatoes, peeled
Salt

1 If necessary, cut potatoes into uniform size.
2 In bottom of large saucepan fitted with vegetable
   steamer, bring 2¹/₂-3¹/₂ cm (1-1¹/₂ inches) of cold
   water to a boil. Add potatoes and sprinkle with
   salt. Cover and steam over high heat about 20
   minutes, or until potatoes can be pierced easily
   with tip of small knife. Cover until ready to serve.
   Reheat if necessary.
3 When ready to serve, remove potatoes from
   steamer and arrange on dinner plates.

Pasta with Fresh Mushroom Sauce
Boston Lettuce, Fennel, and Radicchio Salad

For this Italian-style meal, Jane Salzfass Freiman brings together two effortless dishes: an uncomplicated pasta entrée and a mixed green salad. For the entrée, use either fettuccine or linguine; combine plain pasta with tomato-flavoured pasta if you wish. Mushrooms are the primary ingredient for the lightly seasoned pasta sauce.

The crisp salad offsets the soft textures of the pasta and its sauce. The cook calls for two Italian vegetables: fennel and radicchio. The latter, a ruby-red chicory native to Treviso, Italy, has a slightly bitter but agreeable taste and classically is combined with fennel, which is slightly sweet. Radicchio has a limited winter season, so at other times of the year you can use the familiar red cabbage instead.

What to drink
Here, the classic choice would be a dry, fairly full-bodied white wine: a California Chardonnay or a French Chablis or young Muscadet.

Start-to-Finish Steps
1 Follow pasta recipe step 1.
2 Core lettuce and radicchio, and follow salad recipe step 1.
3 Mince garlic, juice lemon, and mince parsley for pasta. Follow recipe steps 2 through 5.
4 Follow salad recipe steps 2 through 4. Preheat oven to 200 degrees and warm 4 dinner plates in oven.
5 Follow pasta recipe steps 6 through 8.
6 Toss salad, step 5. Remove plates from oven and follow pasta recipe step 9. Serve the salad on separate plates with the pasta.

Tomato-coloured and plain linguine are topped with a sauce of sautéed mushrooms. Serve this dish family style or on individual dinner plates. The three-vegetable salad gains added substance from cheese cubes and ham strips.

Pasta with Fresh Mushroom Sauce

Salt
750 g (1¹/₂ lb) mushrooms
125 ml (4 fl oz) plus 3 tablespoons olive oil
2¹/₂ teaspoons minced garlic
125 ml (4 fl oz) dry white wine
2 teaspoons lemon juice
¹/₄ teaspoon salt
¹/₄ teaspoon freshly ground pepper
2 teaspoons minced parsley
250 g (8 oz) fresh linguine or fettuccine, or 500 g
   (1 lb) total if not using tomato linguine or fettuccine
250 g (8 oz) fresh tomato linguine or fettuccine

1 In covered stockpot or kettle, bring 5 ltrs (8 pts) lightly salted water to a boil.
2 Wipe mushrooms clean with damp paper towels. Slice thinly with chef's knife or in food processor fitted with slicing disc.
3 In 30 cm (12 inch) skillet, heat 4 tablespoons of the olive oil over medium heat. Add garlic and cook until garlic is fragrant, about 2 minutes. Add mushrooms, toss to coat with oil, and continue tossing until mushrooms exude their juices, about 5 minutes.
4 Add white wine, lemon juice, and salt. Bring to a simmer, and cook rapidly until liquid evaporates, about 15 minutes, stirring frequently with wooden spatula.
5 When liquid has evaporated, stir in 4 tablespoons olive oil, pepper, and parsley. Taste for seasoning. The sauce should be slightly salty and peppery. Remove sauce from heat and set aside until pasta is cooked.
6 Add pasta to the boiling water and stir well to combine both pastas. Boil until noodles are tender but still firm, 2 to 4 minutes. Drain immediately in colander.
7 Heat remaining olive oil in pasta pot over low heat. Add noodles and using 2 wooden spoons, toss to coat. Continue tossing until any excess liquid evaporates and noodles begin to separate, 1 to 1¹/₂ minutes.
8 Reheat mushroom sauce over low heat.
9 Divide noodles among warm dinner plates. Top with sauce and serve immediately.

Boston Lettuce, Fennel, and Radicchio Salad

Medium-size head lettuce, cored
Small head radicchio, cored, or 60 g (2 oz) wedge red
   cabbage
Small bulb fennel (about 250 g (8 oz))
125 g (4 oz) mozzarella
60 g (2 oz) good-quality boiled ham, julienned
2 tablespoons sherry vinegar or red wine vinegar
1¹/₂ teaspoons Dijon mustard
Salt and freshly ground pepper
1 tablespoon heavy cream
4 tablespoons olive or vegetable oil

1 Immerse lettuce, radicchio, and fennel in large bowl of cold water. Let stand 5 to 10 minutes, agitating several times to remove any dirt. Drain vegetables in colander and dry in salad spinner or pat dry with paper towels. Wrap vegetables in towel and refrigerate until ready to complete salad.
2 To assemble salad, separate lettuce leaves and tear into bite-size pieces; place leaves in salad bowl. Shred radicchio and add to bowl. Trim and discard fennel stalks; reserve feathery greens for use in salad dressing. Halve fennel bulb, then slice across grain; add fennel slices to bowl.
3 Dice mozzarella and slice ham in julienne strips. Add mozzarella and ham to salad. Cover with cloth towel and refrigerate until ready to serve.
4 Chop fennel greens to make 2 tablespoons. In small bowl or jar, combine vinegar, mustard, and salt and pepper to taste. Mix well with fork or shake jar. Add chopped fennel greens and cream, and mix until blended. Add oil in a slow, steady stream, mixing constantly. If using jar, shake vigorously to combine. Set aside at room temperature.
5 When ready to serve, pour dressing down side of salad bowl, allowing it to run to bottom. Using salad servers or 2 large forks, toss salad thoroughly.

Added touch
Wash, hull, and quarter 500 g (1 lb) of strawberries, then marinate briefly in Grand Marnier or another orange-flavoured liqueur. Serve berries over vanilla ice cream.

Martha Rose Shulman

Menu 1
(*left*)
Saffron Millet
Stir-Fried Tofu with Snow Peas
Hot-and-Sour Cucumber Salad

Martha Rose Shulman learned to appreciate exotic and sophisticated foods when, as a teenager, she travelled throughout Europe and Mexico with her family. In her early twenties, she became a vegetarian because, although she had no philosophical objections to eating meat, she prefered the nutritious, low-fat nature of a well-balanced meatless diet. She quickly discovered that there was plenty of culinary variety open to her. Now a professional cook, she has integrated her quest for good nutrition with her passion for good food. She has spent many years collecting vegetarian recipes from various national cuisines – enough to serve as the foundation for her 'supper club' and catering business and two cookbooks. 'Vegetarianism does not limit anyones choice of foods,' she says. 'Instead, it gives the eager cook an assortment of recipes from every culture.'

To prove her point, she offers three menus with international connections. Menu 1 combines several Asian ingredients (dried black mushrooms, fresh ginger, and tofu) that are stir-fried and served over saffron-flavoured millet – a grain dish similar to rice but a versatile and delicious alternative to it. Menu 2 is a compendium of Mexican dishes ranging from fiery to cold. Menu 3, which calls for wild rice and pumpkin, is distinctly American, although the omelette and curry powder echo other national cuisines as well.

Golden grains of saffron millet are the base for stir-fried tofu, snow peas, black mushrooms, and sliced scallions. The hot-and-sour sliced cucumber salad provides a strong contrast in flavour.

<table>
<tr><td>

</td><td>

Saffron Millet
Stir-Fried Tofu with Snow Peas
Hot-and-Sour Cucumber Salad

</td></tr>
</table>

In this light, non-seasonal dinner, the entrée is stir-fried tofu and vegetables served with millet, a course-ground grain with a nutty flavor. You can buy millet in health-food stores, which usually stock it loose. Like rice and other cereals, millet must be boiled, but sautéing it first, as you do in this recipe, cuts down the time needed for boiling.

Saffron, which colours and flavours the millet, is a pungent and expensive spice that comes from the crocus blossom. Fortunately, a little goes a long way: half a teaspoon is plenty for this dish. Shop for saffron in speciality shops or good supermarkets. If you prefer, substitute turmeric, which is more economical and readily available. It has a musky flavour that will change the taste of the millet dish, but will give it the same golden colour achieved by the use of saffron.

Tofu, or soybean curd, a ubiquitous ingredient in all Asian cooking, comes in a wide range of textures. For stir-frying, buy the firm, Chinese-style variety because it holds its shape. It is a good source of protien and, because it is bland, lends itself to a variety of combinations with other ingredients. Most supermarkets routinely carry it, usually as a dairy item. Refrigerate unused tofu in water in a sealed container. If you change the water daily, tofu will stay fresh a week to 10 days.

The dried mushrooms for the main dish must be softened in water before you add them to other ingredients. Chinese groceries and speciality food shops sell them in 125 g (4 oz) or 250 g (8 oz) plastic or cellophane packages. Wrapped airtight, they last indefinitely. They are excellent in almost any stir-fried dish.

Snow peas should be available at the greengrocer or supermarket year round. Select unblemished, crisp-looking green pods. They will keep a day in a plastic bag in the refrigerator. To string the pods, pinch the stem top and pull the string off along with it. If you can find sugar snap peas, they make a good substitute.

A spoonful of Pernod, the licorice-flavoured French aperitif, adds an unexpected but compatible flavour to the sauce in the main dish. You can substitute any anise-flavoured liqueur or omit it altogether.

Tamari, which both the tofu and the salad recipe call for, is a strong Japanese soy sauce with a deep rich taste. You can find it in health-food stores.

Either a dessert soufflé or a fruit sherbet would provide a refreshing contrast to the highly seasoned, crunchy dishes in this menu.

What to drink
The cook suggests a medium-dry white wine for this meal. A German or domestic Riesling would be a good choice.

Start-to-Finish Steps
1 Follow millet recipe step 1, squeeze enough lemon to measure 1 tablespoon juice, crush saffron threads, if using, in mortar with pestle or in small bowl with back of spoon, and follow step 2.
2 Bring water to a boil and follow stir-fried tofu recipe step 1.
3 For tofu recipe, string snow peas or, if using broccoli, rinse, trim stems, and break broccoli into florets. Trim off scallion roots and any limp green tops; then cut into lengths. Peel and mince garlic clove and enough ginger to measure 2 teaspoons. Cube tofu.
4 Follow tofu recipe steps 2 and 3.
5 Prepare cucumber salad, steps 1 and 2.
6 Follow tofu recipe steps 4 and 5.
7 Remove millet from heat and follow step 3. Follow tofu recipe step 6 and serve with the cucumber salad.

Saffron Millet

625 ml (1¼ pts) vegetable stock or water
2 tablespoons safflower oil
125 g (4 oz) millet
½ teaspoon crushed saffron threads or ground
    turmeric
¼ teaspoon salt
1 tablespoon lemon juice

1   In small saucepan, bring stock or water to a boil.
2   In medium-size, heavy-guage saucepan, heat oil
    over medium heat and sauté millet about 2 minutes,
    until it begins to smell toasty. Pour in stock or
    water and bring to a boil. Stir in saffron or turmeric,
    salt, and lemon juice. Reduce heat, cover, and
    cook 35 to 40 minutes, or until liquid is absorbed.
    Keep covered until ready to serve.
3   Arrange millet along sides of serving platter,
    leaving room in middle for tofu-vegetable mixture.

Stir-Fried Tofu with Snow Peas

8 small or 4 large dried Chinese black mushrooms
2 cups snow peas, strings removed, or broccoli
    florets
3 scallions, cut into 2½ cm (1 inch) lengths
350 g (12 oz) fresh tofu, cut into 2½ cm (1 inch)
    cubes

The sauce:
1 tablespoon cornstarch or arrowroot
60 ml (2 fl oz) water
1 tablespoon dry sherry
1 tablespoon Oriental sesame oil
1 teaspoon honey
1 teaspoon Pernod or other anise-flavored liqueur
2 tablespoons soy sauce, preferably tamari
2 tablespoons safflower oil
1 clove garlic, minced
2 teaspoons finely minced fresh ginger
1 tablespoon soy sauce, preferably tamari

1   Place mushrooms in small bowl and cover with
    boiling water. Let stand 20 to 30 minutes, or until
    soft.
2   Arrange remaining vegetables and tofu in piles on
    large cutting board or place on seperate plates.
3   In small bowl, combine sauce ingredients and set
    aside.
4   When mushrooms have softened, remove from
    soaking liquid and rinse with cold water to dislodge
    any grit trapped in gills. Squeeze out excess liquid

and reserve. Remove tough stems and cut
mushrooms into strips. Over small bowl, pour
soaking liquid through strainer lined with
cheesecloth or paper towels and reserve.

5   In wok or large, heavy-guage skillet, heat safflower
    oil over medium heat until hot. Add garlic and
    ginger, and sauté, stirring with wooden spoon or
    Chinese metal wok spatula, for 10 seconds. Add
    tofu and soy sauce, and stir-fry 1 minute. Add
    mushrooms and snow peas or broccoli and stir-fry
    another 1 to 2 minutes. Pour in reserved mushroom
    liquid, cover, and simmer 3 to 5 minutes, or until
    vegetables are crisp-tender. Add scallions. Stir
    sauce mixture, making sure cornstarch is dissolved,
    and add to the vegetables. Cook, stirring, until
    sauce thickens and glazes the vegetables.
6   Remove from heat and mound mixture in middle
    of serving platter surrounded by saffron millet.

Hot and Sour Cucumber Salad

3 tablespoons white wine vinegar or apple cider
    vinegar
1 tablespoon mild-flavoured honey, such as acacia,
    clover, or lavendar
1 tablespoon soy sauce, preferably tamari
⅛ to ¼ teaspoon Cayenne pepper, or ½ teaspoon
    hot pepper flakes
¼ teaspoon freshly ground pepper
3 tablespoons safflower oil
1 tablespoon Oriental sesame oil
2 large cucumbers
2 tablespoons minced scallions

1   To prepare dressing, combine all ingredients in
    salad bowl except cucumbers and scallions. Stir
    well to combine.
2   Peel cucumbers and slice very thinly. Toss
    cucumbers with dressing and minced scallions.
    Cover and refrigerate until ready to serve.

Leftover suggestions

If you bought a large block of tofu, you may have
some left over. Add it to omelettes, scrambled eggs,
soups, salads, or stir-fried rice. Add vegetables, diced
meat, or even fruit and nuts to leftover millet for
another stir-fried meal.

Chilies con Queso (Chilies with Cheese Fondue)
Spanish Rice
Guacamole Chalupas

Chilies con queso, a Mexican-style cheese fondue, is eaten with a variety of dippers: carrots, courgettes, red peppers and tostada chips. The hearty side dishes are Spanish rice and chalupas, a salad layered on crisp tortillas.

The main dish here is melted cheese spiked with hot chilies and flavoured with onion, tomatoes, and beer – a lively Mexican version of a Swiss fondue. *Chalupas*, 'little boats,' are crisp corn tortillas filled with salad. Canned green *jalapeño* and *serrano* chilies are easy to find in supermarkets that carry Mexican ingredients, but *chipotles* may be hard to find.

What to drink
For this menu, choose a dark Mexican beer or a simple Côtes du Rhône or California Zinfandel.

Start-to-Finish Steps
At least 30 minutes ahead: If using frozen tortillas for chalupas, remove from the freezer and unwrap. Do not try to separate still-frozen tortillas.

1. Prepare the vegetables for all three recipes.
2. Follow chilies con queso recipe steps 1 through 4.
3. Follow Spanish rice recipe steps 1 through 6.
4. While rice is cooking, juice lemon, grate cheese for chilies and for chalupas in food processor fitted with grating disc or with cheese grater, and follow chalupas recipe steps 1 through 3. Preheat oven to 200 degrees.
5. Follow chilies con queso recipe step 5.
6. Follow chalupas recipe step 4.
7. Turn rice into serving bowl. Follow chilies con queso recipe step 6, chalupas recipe step 5, and serve with the rice.

Chilies con Queso

1 medium-size courgette, sliced lengthwise into
   spears
3 canned whole jalapeño or chipotle peppers
1 tablespoon cornstarch
2 tablespoons beer or water
1 tablespoon safflower oil
1/2 medium-size onion, chopped
1 clove garlic, minced
2 ripe tomatoes, peeled, seeded, and chopped
125 ml (4 fl oz) beer
2 cups grated Gruyère cheese (about 250 g (8 oz))
2 carrots, scraped and sliced lengthwise into spears
2 green bell peppers, cored, seeded, and sliced
   lengthwise into thick strips
1/2 red bell pepper, cored, seeded, and sliced
   lengthwise into thick strips
Tostada chips

1 In medium-size saucepan, bring 750 ml (1 1/2 pts)
   of water to a boil. Add courgette and blanch 1
   minute. Drain in colander and refresh under cold
   running water. Wrap in paper towels and refrigerate
   until ready to serve.
2 Seed and slice jalapeño or chipotle peppers. (*Note:*
   The capsaicin in the pepper veins and seeds can
   be extremely irritating to eyes and lips, so wash
   hands thoroughly immediately after handling
   peppers.)
3 Dissolve cornstarch in 2 tablespoons of beer or
   water.
4 In same saucepan used for courgettes, heat oil
   over medium heat. Add onion and garlic, and
   sauté until onion is translucent. Add jalapeño
   peppers and tomatoes, stir, and cook 2 minutes
   over medium heat.
5 Add beer to the tomato mixture and bring to a
   simmer. Slowly add cheese by handfuls, stirring
   until melted. Then gradually add cornstarch mixture,
   stirring until sauce is thick and smooth. Transfer

sauce con queso to chafing dish or fondue pot and
keep hot over low flame.
6 Remove courgette from refrigerator. Arrange
   courgette, carrots, peppers, and tostada chips on
   platter, ready for dipping into hot cheese sauce.

Spanish Rice

500 ml (1 pt) chicken or vegetable stock
1 to 2 tablespoons safflower oil
1/2 medium-size onion, chopped
2 cloves garlic, minced
1/2 green bell pepper, cored, seeded, and sliced
   lengthwise into strips
1/2 red bell pepper, cored, seeded, and sliced
   lengthwise into strips
2 ripe tomatoes, peeled, seeded, and chopped
175 g (6 oz) long-grain rice
125 ml (4 fl oz) dry white wine
1/2 teaspoon crushed saffron threads or ground
   turmeric
Salt
Freshly ground pepper

1 In small saucepan, bring stock to a simmer.
2 In large, heavy-bottomed sauté pan, heat safflower
   oil over medium heat and sauté onion and garlic
   until onion begins to soften, about 2 minutes.
3 Add peppers and tomatoes and sauté 2 minutes.
4 Add rice and sauté, stirring, about 2 minutes.
5 Add wine and cook, stirring, until wine has almost
   evaporated.
6 Crush saffron threads, if using. Add saffron or
   turmeric and hot stock to pan, stir, and simmer,
   uncovered, over medium-low heat 20 to 25 minutes,
   or until liquid is absorbed and rice is *al dente*.
   Season to taste, and keep covered until ready to
   serve.

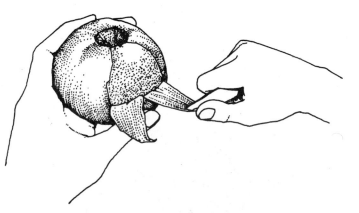

Pull skin from cored tomato with sharp paring knife.

Squeeze seeds out with one hand.

Guacamole Chalupas

1 to 2 canned serrano or jalapeño peppers
3 small or 2 large ripe avocados, preferably the dark, knobby Haas variety
3 ripe tomatoes, peeled, seeded, and chopped
1 small onion, minced
1 clove garlic, minced
Juice of $1/2$ to 1 lemon
Salt
Ground cumin
Chili powder
2 to 3 tablespoons chopped cilantro
1 tablespoon vinegar
Safflower oil
8 corn tortillas, fresh or frozen
125 g (4 oz) Cheddar cheese, grated
500 ml (1 pt) plain, low-fat yogurt
125 g (4 oz) alfalfa sprouts
30 g (1 oz) shelled sunflower seeds (optional)

1 Seed, devein, and chop peppers. (*Note:* The capsaicin in the pepper veins and seeds can be extremely irritating to eyes and lips, so wash hands thoroughly immediately after handling peppers.)

2 Cut avocados in half, remove pits, and scoop flesh out into medium-size serving bowl. Mash together avocados, one third of the chopped tomatoes, 2 tablespoons of the minced onion, and garlic. Season guacamole to taste with lemon juice, salt, cumin, and chili powder. Cover and refrigerate until ready to serve.

3 In another medium-size serving bowl, toss remaining chopped tomatoes and onion with chopped hot peppers, chopped cilantro, vinegar, and salt to taste. Cover and refrigerate. Line a heatproof platter with a triple layer of paper towels.

4 Add just enough oil to 25 cm (10 inch) skillet to coat bottom. Heat the oil over medium heat until hot. Add 1 tortilla and cook about 20 to 30 seconds on 1 side. Using tongs, carefully turn tortilla and cook another 20 to 30 seconds on the other side, or just until golden and crisp. Transfer to paper-towel-lined platter to drain. Repeat with remaining tortillas, adding more oil as necessary. Keep tortillas warm in oven until ready to serve.

5 Remove tortillas from oven and serve on a platter with the guacamole, tomato sauce, cheese, yogurt, sprouts, and sunflower seeds. Or serve tortillas plain, and let guests assemble their own combinations.

Making Stock

Although canned chicken broth or stock is all right for emergencies, homemade chicken stock has a rich flavour that is hard to match. Moreover, the commercial broths – particularly the canned ones – are likely to be oversalted.

To make your own stock, save chicken parts as they accumulate and put them in a bag in the freezer; then have a rainy-day stock-making session, using the recipe below. The skin from a yellow onion will add colour; the optional veal bone will add extra flavour and richness to the stock.

Basic Chicken Stock

1.4 Kg (3 lb) bony chicken parts, such as wings, back, and neck
1 veal knuckle (optional)
$3^1/_2$ ltrs (6 pts) cold water
1 yellow unpeeled onion, stuck with 2 cloves
2 stalks celery with leaves, cut in two
12 crushed peppercorns
2 carrots, scraped and cut into 5 cm (2 inch) lengths
4 sprigs parsley
1 bay leaf
1 tablespoon fresh thyme, or 1 teaspoon dried
salt (optional)

1 Wash chicken parts and veal knuckle (if you are using it) thoroughly under cold running water. Place in large soup kettle or stockpot (any big pot) with the remaining ingredients – except salt. Cover pot and bring to a boil over medium heat.

2 Lower heat and simmer stock, partly covered, 2 to 3 hours. Skim foam and scum from top of stock several times. Add salt to taste after stock has cooked 1 hour.

3 Strain stock through fine sieve placed over large bowl. Discard solids. Let stock cool uncovered (this will speed cooling process). When completely cool, refrigerate. Fat will rise and congeal conveniently at top. You may skim it off and discard it or leave it as a protective covering.

Puffed Broccoli Omelettes
Wild Rice with Almonds
Curried Pumpkin Purée

The grain dish in this meal, an ideal brunch for guests, is wild rice. The seeds of a wild grass, wild rice is harvested by hand. Hence, it is always in short supply and always expensive. However, 175 g (6 oz) of wild rice will serve four. Good supermarkets and speciality food stores sell it in boxes. Adding almonds, onion, and sherry, as in this recipe, greatly enhances its earthy flavour.

Omelettes are easy to make and so versatile that they appear, in some form, in almost every national cuisine. Almost any vegetable, meat, or cheese filling

is good with an omelette. The trick is to keep the eggs from sticking to the pan, so that you can fold them over the filling. Use a nonstick skillet, as in this recipe, or a well-seasoned pan that you use only for omelettes and scrambled eggs. Never allow it to overheat. For puffed omelettes, which look like soufflés and take two minutes to make, beat the whites and yolks separately. The whites must be stiff and the yolks thick and pale.

If you use fresh pumpkin for the purée, buy a 1 Kg (2 lb) pumpkin that is bright orange and feels heavy

Puffy golden broccoli omelettes are accompanied by a curried pumpkin casserole and wild rice.

for its size. You can substitute canned pumpkin, if you wish. You can also use other winter squashes, such as butternut or acorn. Handle them the same way.

What to drink
An uncomplicated wine would be the best choice here. If you want red, select a simple California Gamay; if you prefer white, choose an Italian Pinot Bianco or Pinot Grigio.

Start-to-Finish Steps
One hour before meal: Remove eggs from refrigerator.

1   Wash rice in colander and follow wild rice recipe step 1.
2   As rice simmers, follow pumpkin purée recipe step 1.
3   Follow broccoli omelettes recipe steps 1 and 2, using same saucepan and steamer used for pumpkin.
4   Slice enough almonds to measure 1 tablespoon and coarsely chop remaining almonds. Follow rice recipe step 2. Reduce oven temperature to 200 degrees.
5   Grate fresh ginger, if using, and follow pumpkin purée recipe steps 2 through 4.
6   Grate cheese for omelettes. Dice onion and chop almonds, and mince garlic for wild rice. Follow rice recipe steps 3 and 4.
7   Prepare omelettes, steps 3 through 6. Serve with pumpkin purée and wild rice.

Puffed Broccoli Omelettes

6 eggs, at room temperature
1 bunch broccoli
Salt and freshly ground pepper
30 g (1 oz) freshly grated Parmesan cheese (optional)
4 tablespoons unsalted butter

1   Separate eggs, dividing yolks between 2 medium-size bowls and placing all the whites in 1 large bowl.
2   Wash and trim broccoli and separate enough into florets to measure 250 g (8 oz). In saucepan fitted with vegetable steamer, steam the florets over 2½ cm (1 inch) of water 10 minutes. Drain in colander. Chop half the florets; set aside the remainder.
3   Beat whites until stiff but not dry.
4   Beat 3 yolks and add salt and freshly ground

pepper to taste. Using rubber spatula, gently fold in one third of whites, then fold in half the remaining whites, half the chopped broccoli, and 2 tablespoons of the cheese, if using.
5   In 22-25 cm (9-10 inch) nonstick skillet, heat 2 tablespoons of the butter over medium heat. When butter has sizzled, gently pour in egg mixture. Tilt pan to distribute mixture evenly and cook 1 minute. Arrange half the whole florets on one side of the omelette and cook 1 more minute. With plastic spatula, carefully fold omelette over broccoli-lined half as you turn it out onto platter.
6   Follow steps 4 and 5 for preparing second omelette. Turn onto platter, beside first omelette. Serve at once.

Wild Rice with Almonds

500 ml (1 pt) vegetable or chicken stock, or water
175 g (6 oz) wild rice, washed
1 tablespoon sliced almonds for garnish (optional)
2 tablespoons safflower oil or butter, or 1 tablespoon each
Small onion, diced
1 clove garlic, minced
45 g (1½ oz) coarsely chopped almonds
2 tablespoons dry sherry
1 tablespoon soy sauce

1   In medium-size saucepan, bring stock or water to a boil and slowly stir in wild rice. Return to a boil. Reduce heat, cover, and simmer 45 minutes, or until tender and liquid is absorbed. Keep covered until ready to use.
2   Preheat oven to 200°C (400°F or Mark 6). Place sliced almonds on baking sheet and toast in oven about 3 to 5 minutes, or until golden. Set aside.
3   In large sauté pan, heat 1 tablespoon of the oil or butter over medium heat and sauté onion and garlic until onion is translucent. Add chopped almonds and sauté 1 minute.
4   Add remaining oil or butter and stir in cooked wild rice. Cook, stirring, 1 to 2 minutes. Add sherry and soy sauce. Toss rice over medium heat 1 to 2 minutes. Transfer to serving dish, garnish with toasted sliced almonds, and keep warm in oven until ready to serve.

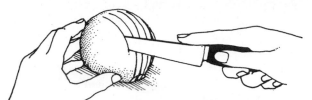

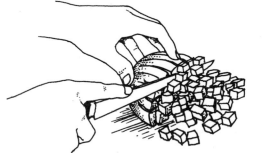

Hold onion half flat on cutting surface; make vertical cuts with small chef's knife.

Make horizontal cuts to form a crosshatch pattern.

Slice perpendicularly to cutting surface; onion will fall into dice.

Curried Pumpkin Purée

1 Kg (2 lb) pumpkin
1 tablespoon unsalted butter
1/2 teaspoon grated fresh ginger, or 1/4 teaspoon
   ground ginger
1 1/2 to 2 teaspoons curry powder
2 tablespoons plain yogurt, crème fraîche, or sour
   cream
Salt
Freshly ground pepper

1   Quarter, seed, and peel pumpkin. Cut into small cubes. You will need about 350 g (12 oz). In saucepan fitted with steamer, steam pumpkin 15 minutes, or until tender. Drain in colander.
2   Purée pumpkin in food processor or put through food mill.
3   In another saucepan, melt butter. Add ginger and curry powder, and sauté, stirring, over low heat, 2 to 3 minutes.
4   Add pumpkin, yogurt, and salt and pepper to taste to mixture in saucepan, and stir to combine. Transfer to serving dish, cover loosely with foil, and keep warm in oven until ready to serve.

Added touch
Fresh fruit is a satisfying dessert with this meal – try sliced pears, apples, or bananas, raw or poached. A dried-fruit compote also would complement this menu.

Peter Kump

Menu 1
(Right)
Fresh Beetroot Salad
Tomato and Onion Salad
Carrot and Horseradish Salad
Turkey Scallops with Brown
Butter and Caper Sauce
Green Beans with Sweet-and-Sour Sauce

Austrians have always loved good food, particularly elaborate pastries. At the turn of the century, Viennese cooks could match their French counterparts dish for dish, but when the Empire collapsed, interest in elaborate recipes declined. Today, Austrian cooking is enjoying a renaissance.

Because Peter Kump is of Austrian descent, he has been especially curious about that country's food and has travelled there often to learn how to prepare authentic dishes. At his cooking school, he teaches Austrian techniques and recreates fine Old Empire dishes for his friends.

Menu 1 is a sampling of what an Austrian family might plan for an autumn dinner. Unlike the French, Austrians often serve several small salads to lighten otherwise rich, heavy meals, changing salad ingredients seasonally. Peter Kump mixes grated raw beetroot with minced onion, sour cream, and caraway seeds; thinly sliced tomatoes with a sprinkling of minced onions (the vinaigrette tenderizes the onions); and grated carrots with grated horseradish, a very important Austrian seasoning. The turkey scallops are dipped in beaten eggs and bread crumbs, sautéed, then served with a brown butter and caper sauce.

Vegetables are among Peter Kump's favourite ingredients. In Menu 2, he uses celeriac, a popular European root vegetable, and serves it in a salad with apples. In Menu 3, he serves fish fillets with grated courgettes, sliced, roasted red peppers, and minced shallots.

Three colourful vegetable salads – grated fresh beetroot, sliced tomatoes with minced onions, and grated carrots and horseradish – are unusual accompaniments to this Austrian-influenced meal. Present the turkey scallops and the green beans on the same platter.

Fresh Beetroot Salad/Tomato and Onion Salad/Carrot and Horseradish Salad
Turkey Scallops with Brown Butter and Caper Sauce
Green Beans with Sweet-and-Sour Sauce

Peter Kump stresses that, with proper planning, you can assemble this multicourse meal with minimal fuss. Streamline your work by first mincing all the ingredients needed for the recipes.

Turkey scallops – thinly sliced turkey breast – cook quickly, so sauté them just before you are ready to serve the meal. Most supermarkets now package fresh turkey breasts, whole or sliced into scallops. If your market stocks only whole breasts, ask the butcher to slice the meat into 1 cm (¹/₂ inch) thick scallops. Thinly sliced chicken breasts make a good substitute.

What to drink

The cook favours an Austrian white wine to match these dishes: if available, choose a Grüner Veltliner. If not, try an Alsatian Sylvaner or Riesling.

Start-to-Finish Steps

1   Mince yellow onions, chives, and scallions, if using, for salads. Mince parsley for carrot salad and for turkey. Mince capers for turkey and white onion for green beans.
2   Squeeze 2 or 3 lemons to make 6 tablespoons lemon juice for beetroot salad and carrot salad.
3   Prepare beetroot salad, steps 1 and 2.
4   Follow tomato and onion salad recipe steps 1 and 2.
5   Follow carrot salad recipe steps 1 and 2.
6   For green beans recipe, trim beans and follow steps 1 and 2.
7   Trim crusts from bread and, using processor or grater, make crumbs. With chef's knife, slice turkey breast into 4 scallops and follow recipe steps 1 and 2.
8   Follow green beans recipe step 3.
9   Follow turkey recipe step 4.
10 Preheat oven to 200 degrees. Follow green beans recipe steps 4 and 5.
11 In preheated oven, warm serving platter for turkey and bowl for green beans.
12 Follow turkey recipe steps 5 and 6.
13 Follow green beans recipe step 6.
14 Follow turkey recipe steps 7 and 8, tomato and onion salad step 3, and carrot salad step 3. Serve turkey scallops with the green beans and salads.

Fresh Beetroot Salad

6 medium-size beetroot (about 750 g (1¹/₂ lb) total weight)
3 tablespoons lemon juice
¹/₂ teaspoon salt
Pinch of sugar
1 tablespoon minced yellow onion
1 tablespoon minced chives or scallion greens
6 tablespoons sour cream
2 teaspoons caraway seeds, crushed

1   Wash beets well. Trim tops, peel, and rinse beetroot. Using food processor or grater, grate finely.
2   Mix remaining ingredients in salad bowl. Add grated beetroot, cover, and macerate for about 45 minutes.

Tomato and Onion Salad

3 medium-size ripe tomatoes
1 small yellow onion, minced
¹/₄ teaspoon salt
Freshly ground pepper
4 tablespoons olive oil
2 tablespoons white wine vinegar
1 tablespoon minced chives for garnish

1   Rinse tomatoes and slice thinly. Place in salad bowl and sprinkle with minced onion, salt, and pepper to taste.
2   In small bowl, mix oil and vinegar, and pour over tomatoes; toss gently. Cover and chill at least 30 minutes, stirring gently once or twice.
3   Just before serving, sprinkle with minced chives.

Carrot and Horseradish Salad

3¹/₂ cm (1¹/₂ inch) piece of fresh horseradish, or
   2 tablespoons bottled white horseradish
4 medium-size carrots
3 tablespoons lemon juice
¹/₂ teaspoon salt
Pinch of sugar
1 tablespoon minced yellow onion
2 teaspoons minced chives
1 tablespoon plus 1 teaspoon minced parsley
1 to 2 teaspoons Dijon mustard
6 tablespoons sour cream

1 If using horseradish, peel and then grate in food processor or with grater. Peel carrots, trim ends, and halve lengthwise. Slice into quarters and grate.

2 In salad bowl, combine remaining ingredients, except 1 teaspoon parsley, and toss with the carrots and horseradish. Cover and refrigerate until ready to serve.

3 Just before serving, sprinkle with reserved parsley.

Turkey Scallops with Brown Butter and Caper Sauce

100 g (3 oz) flour
150 g (5 oz) fresh dry bread crumbs
2 large eggs
1 teaspoon safflower oil
Dash of salt and freshly ground pepper
750 g (1¹/₂ lb) turkey breast, sliced into 4 large
   scallops
175 g (6 oz) unsalted butter
2 tablespoons minced parsley
2 tablespoons minced capers
4 tablespoons white wine vinegar

1 Place flour and bread crumbs on 2 sheets of wax paper.

2 In shallow dish or pie plate, beat eggs with oil, 1 tablespoon of water, and a dash of salt and pepper.

3 Dry turkey scallops with paper towels. Dip 1 scallop at a time in the flour and coat well. Shake off excess, then, with one hand, gently slide scallop into egg mixture.

4 With other hand, pick up egg-coated scallop and let excess drain off. Finally, dip scallop in crumbs, turning once, and pat with same hand, making sure scallop is evenly coated. Shake off excess and place on large, flat plate. Continue until all the scallops are breaded. Chill scallops in refrigerator until ready to cook.

5 In large sauté pan, heat half the butter over medium heat. When butter turns a hazelnut colour, add scallops in single layer. Sauté 3 minutes on first side, then, using metal spatula, turn and sauté about 2 minutes on second. When done, remove scallops to warm serving platter.

6 With slotted metal spoon, carefully remove any burned bits from pan and add remaining butter. Over medium heat, cook butter until it begins to turn colour, but do not let it burn. Remove pan from heat. Cool slightly before stirring in parsley and capers.

7 Add vinegar to sauté pan and over high heat rapidly boil it down to 1 tablespoon, scraping up any remaining brown. Add to butter sauce.

8 To serve, spoon sauce over scallops.

Green Beans with Sweet-and-Sour Sauce

2 tablespoons unsalted butter
1 white onion, minced
500 g (1 lb) young green beans, trimmed
175 ml (6 fl oz) beef stock
2 whole cloves
Salt
1 tablespoon white wine vinegar
1 teaspoon sugar

1 In medium-size sauté pan, melt butter and sauté onion over medium heat until browned, about 8 to 10 minutes.

2 In large covered saucepan, bring 3¹/₂ ltrs (6 pts) of water to a boil.

3 Add stock and cloves to the onions, and simmer 10 minutes, until sauce is reduced and thick.

4 Add ¹/₄ teaspoon salt, vinegar, and sugar to sauce and stir to blend. Turn off heat and cover.

5 Add 1 tablespoon salt, and beans to boiling water. Cook beans about 8 to 10 minutes, or until cooked through but still crisp. Drain and refresh under cold running water.

6 Just before serving, add beans to sauce and simmer gently 3 to 5 minutes. Turn into heated serving bowl.

Celeriac Winter Salad
Chicken Piccata
Braised Fresh Spinach and Mushrooms

Celeriac and apple salad, together with mushrooms braised lightly with spinach, provide interesting colour and texture next to chicken piccata – sautéed chicken cutlets – garnished here with lemon slices and parsley sprigs.

This winter meal starts off with a sweet-and-sour salad of raw apples and celeriac – celery root – either grated or cut into fine julienne strips and marinated in a tenderizing homemade mayonnaise. Whole fresh celeriac looks lumpy and bewhiskered, but it tastes like a very flavourful celery and combines well with other raw vegetables. Good greengrocers and many supermarkets now stock celeriac. Buy roots that are no thicker than 10 cm (4 inches) in diameter – otherwise the flesh may be woody. To prepare celeriac, remove the roots and leafy tops and scrub the tough outer skin. Then, with a paring knife, peel off the skin as if you were peeling citrus fruit. Since its skin is very thick you will need to trim away almost half the root. To prevent the flesh from darkening when exposed to air, sprinkle it with lemon juice, as Peter Kump suggests. You can use regular celery when celeriac is out of season.

For the braised spinach and mushrooms, coarsely chop the spinach leaves before cooking. This will make the spinach easier to eat.

What to drink

A full-bodied, dry white wine with plenty of character is in order here: a California Chardonnay or Sauvignon Blanc. The next best choice would be a very light red, perhaps a Beaujolais Nouveau.

Start-to-Finish Steps

1 Preheat oven to 400 degrees.
2 Squeeze 2 lemons into small bowl to make 4 tablespoons juice and follow celeriac salad recipe steps 1 through 3.
3 Follow braised spinach recipe steps 1 and 2.
4 Follow celeriac salad recipe steps 4 and 5.
5 Follow spinach recipe steps 3 and 4, and grate nutmeg.
6 Follow chicken piccata recipe steps 1 and 2. Squeeze 1 lemon into small cup; slice the other thinly for garnish. Place serving dish and platter in oven to warm briefly.
7 Follow chicken recipe steps 3 through 5, spinach recipe step 5, celeriac salad recipe step 6, and serve.

Celeriac Winter Salad

1 small knob celeriac
Salt
4 tablespoons lemon juice
1 red apple, preferably Delicious
1 green apple
60 g (2 oz) slivered almonds
1 large egg
2 tablespoons Dijon mustard
Freshly ground pepper
250 ml (8 fl oz) vegetable oil, preferably safflower

1 Peel celeriac, cut into thin slices, and then into fine julienne strips. Or, grate in food processor fitted with metal blade. Place celeriac in small bowl and sprinkle with 2 teaspoons salt and 2 tablespoons of lemon juice; set aside.
2 Core and quarter apples, but do not peel them. Cut them into fine julienne strips, or grate them in food processor or by hand. Wrap in damp cloth and refrigerate until ready to use.
3 Place almonds on baking sheet and toast in preheated oven about 3 to 4 minutes, or until golden. Remove from oven and set aside until ready to use. Set oven at 170°C (325°F or Mark 3).
4 If using food processor, wipe clean. Combine egg (if making mayonnaise by hand, use only the yolk), mustard, remaining lemon juice, pinch of salt, and freshly ground pepper to taste in processor or large bowl. With processor running slowly or while whisking vigorously with wire whisk, add oil in a slow, steady stream until mayonnaise thickens and holds together.
5 Rinse celery root in colander to remove salt and pat dry with paper towels. Transfer to serving bowl, add the mustard-mayonnaise and toss well. Set aside.
6 Stir in the apple and the almonds, and serve.

Chicken Piccata

2 whole skinless, boneless chicken breasts
4 tablespoons unsalted butter
125 ml (4 fl oz) chicken stock
2 lemons, 1 freshly squeezed and 1 sliced for garnish (optional)
Salt
Freshly ground pepper
Sprigs of curly parsley for garnish (optional)

1 Halve chicken breasts and remove small mignon from underside of each of the 4 pieces. The mignon is about 2½ cm (1 inch) wide at its widest point and about 10 cm (4 inches) long. Simply pull them from the breast halves; set aside.
2 Place the larger pieces of chicken on a cutting board and, with a chef's knife, cut each piece in half horizontally. You will end up with 8 cutlets and 4 mignons.
3 In sauté pan large enough to hold all the chicken in a single layer (or you can cook them in 2 batches) heat 2 tablespoons of the butter over medium heat. While butter is heating, dry cutlets with paper towels – do this just before them in pan. Then sauté cutlets 1 minute on each side. Using slotted metal spatula, transfer them directly to warm serving platter while completing sauce.
4 Add chicken stock to pan. Turn heat to high, scraping up any brown bits, and reduce stock by a little more than half. Add lemon juice and salt and pepper to taste, and cook another minute. Remove from heat and swirl in remaining 2 tablespoons butter until it is incorporated and sauce appears velvety.
5 Spoon the sauce over chicken, coating it well. Garnish with lemon slices and parsley sprigs, if desired.

Braised Fresh Spinach and Mushrooms

750 g (1½ lb) spinach
1 medium-size onion
250 g (8 oz) thinly sliced mushrooms
5 tablespoons butter
125 ml (4 fl oz) chicken stock
Salt
Freshly ground pepper
Freshly ground nutmeg

1 In large bowl, clean spinach thoroughly in several changes of cool water. Discard tough stems and any wilted leaves, and chop. Peel and chop onion. Wipe mushrooms clean with damp paper towels and slice thinly.
2 In casserole, melt 3 tablespoons of the butter over medium-low heat. Add onion and sauté 4 to 5 minutes, until translucent but not browned. Add mushrooms and sauté another minute.
3 Turn heat to high, add stock, and bring to a boil.
4 Add spinach to casserole by handfuls, stirring constantly. Cover casserole and place in oven; bake 20 minutes.
5 Using slotted metal spoon, remove vegetables to heated serving dish. Put casserole on stove and over high heat reduce liquid to 2 tablespoons. Add remaining butter and a large pinch each of salt, pepper, and nutmeg. Pour over vegetables, toss well, and correct seasonings.

Menu 3

Cream of Lemon Soup
Fillets of Sole with Courgettes and Peppers
Blueberry Cream-Cheese Parfaits

Only fresh lemon juice can give the creamy soup in this menu its sparkling clean flavour. Do not substitute bottled or frozen juice. A cautionary note: instead of pouring the beaten yolks directly into the hot chicken stock, which would scramble them, first add a little of the hot stock to the yolks, stirring constantly to avoid any lumpiness. Add a second ladleful of stock, continuing to stir. This heats the yolks through gently so they can be incorporated more easily with the stock.

Fillets of fresh sole or flounder, flattened to 5 mm (¼ inch), bake quickly in a hot oven. You can cook the fillets in a baking pan or, as Peter Kump suggests, in stoneware or heatproof dinnerware. Before baking, spread mild, grainy mustard on both sides of the fillets. The grains, actually mustard seeds, add flavour and texture to the fillets without overpowering the delicate taste of the fish. When you shop, choose fish with firm, moist, odourless flesh. Store the fish well-wrapped in plastic or foil in the refrigerator and use it the same day.

The courgette and red pepper mixture, sautéed quickly, is a colourful accompaniment to the fish and a nice contrast in texture.

The blueberry parfaits, which are part of the meal rather than an **Added touch**, can be made with the other two dishes in under an hour. They taste like feathery-light cheesecake, and take only minutes to prepare. Peter Kump advises you to use only pure maple syrup rather than the blended or flavoured syrups, because nothing matches the distinctive, delicate flavour of the pure syrup. When fresh blueberries are not in season, use frozen strawberries or raspberries in their own juice or orange sections soaked in orange-flavoured liqueur. If you opt for the liqueur, eliminate the maple syrup.

What to drink
Muscadet, a bone-dry white, is a classic accompaniment to fish dishes like this one. A crisp Italian white wine, such as Verdicchio, is also compatible.

Start-to-Finish Steps
One hour ahead: Remove cream cheese from refrigerator.

1 Place medium-size bowl in refrigerator to chill. Follow fillets of sole recipe steps 1 and 2.
2 Follow blueberry parfait recipe steps 1 through 4.
3 Butter baking dish, chop shallots, and grate nutmeg. Follow fillets of sole recipe steps 3 through 6.
4 Prepare lemon soup recipe steps 1 through 5 and serve.
5 Follow fillets of sole recipe steps 7 through 9 and serve.
6 For dessert, follow blueberry parfait recipe step 5.

Cream of Lemon Soup

2 lemons
500 ml (1 pt) chicken stock
250 ml (8 fl oz) heavy cream
3 egg yolks
Salt
Freshly ground pepper
4 sprigs parsley for garnish (optional)

1 Cut 4 thin slices from 1 lemon. Squeeze juice from leftover lemon and from second one into small bowl.
2 In large saucepan, heat chicken stock until warm. Stir in cream. Turn off heat, cover, and keep warm.
3 In small bowl, lightly beat egg yolks with 2 tablespoons of the lemon juice. Pour in a ladleful of hot soup, stirring constantly. Repeat with another ladleful of soup.
4 Then, stirring constantly, pour yolk-lemon mixture into soup.
5 Taste for seasoning, adding additional lemon juice, salt, and pepper to heighten flavour, if desired. Ladle into soup bowls, float a lemon slice in each bowl, and garnish with parsley sprig, if desired.

Creamy lemon soup, garnished with sliced lemon and parsley, introduces the mustard-coated fillets of sole and the grated courgette and red peppers. Follow this light meal with rich blueberry parfaits.

Fillets of Sole with Courgettes and Peppers

4 small courgettes
1 teaspoon salt
2 red bell peppers
750 g-1 Kg (1½ to 2 lb) fresh fillets of sole or flounder
4 teaspoons coarse-grained French mustard, such as Moutarde de Meaux
3 tablespoons unsalted butter
2 shallots, peeled and chopped
Freshly grated nutmeg
Freshly ground pepper

1 Scrub courgettes well, cut off ends and discard; grate in food processor or with large holes of grater. Place grated courgettes in colander, toss with salt to mix evenly, and set over plate to drain at least 15 minutes.

2 Scorch red peppers by setting them directly over gas flame or under oven broiler, turning them with tongs until all sides are blistered and black. Place in a paper bag for 5 to 10 minutes.

3 With large, wet chef's knife, flatten fish skillets so that they are of even thickness, preferably about 5 mm (¼ inch) thick. Cut into serving pieces and, using rubber spatula, spread with mustard on both

59

sides. Arrange in single layer in buttered ovenproof non-aluminium baking dish.

4 Preheat oven to 220°C (425°F or Mark 7).

5 Remove peppers from bag and peel them under running water. Slice open, remove seeds and ribs, and julienne. Set aside.

6 By handfuls, thoroughly squeeze all liquid from courgettes.

7 Bake fillets 4 to 6 minutes.

8 While fish is baking, melt butter over medium heat in medium-size sauté pan. Add shallots and sauté about 1 minute, or until translucent. Add courgettes and sauté another 2 minutes. Season to taste with freshly grated nutmeg and pepper. Add red pepper strips and continue to sauté 2 to 3 minutes.

9 With metal spatula, transfer fish fillets to dinner plates and serve with courgette and red pepper mixture on the side.

Blueberry Cream-Cheese Parfaits

500 g (1 lb) blueberries
125 ml (4 fl oz) pure maple syrup
125 g (4 oz) fresh cream cheese, at room temperature
60 g (2 oz) confectioners' sugar
1 teaspoon vanilla extract
250 ml (8 fl oz) heavy cream, well chilled
Maple syrup for garnish (optional)

1 Pick over blueberries, carefully removing stems and any bruised or overripe fruit. Rinse well in strainer, drain, and transfer to medium-size bowl, reserving a few berries for garnish. Add maple syrup to bowl and stir to combine.

2 Using hand mixer, blend cream cheese with sugar and vanilla in large mixing bowl.

3 In chilled medium-size bowl whip cream until soft peaks form. Carefully fold cream into cream-cheese mixture just until combined. Fold in blueberries with syrup.

4 Divide mixture among 4 parfait glasses and refrigerate.

5 When ready to serve, garnish with reserved blueberries and drizzle on a little maple syrup, if desired.

Meet the Cooks

Madhur Jaffrey

Madhur Jaffrey, born in Delhi, India, went to America as an actress and then became a writer and cookery teacher. She has written for numerous magazines and is the author of various cookery titles. Madhur Jaffrey is particularly well known through her BBC television cookery series.

Marlene Sorosky

Born and raised in Oregon, Marlene Sorosky studied classical cooking in France, and then continued her culinary education in the United States with a number of noted professional chefs. Now living in California, she is the author of *Cookery for Entertaining* and *Marlene Sorosky's Year Round Holiday Cookbook*.

Beverly Cox

Beverly Cox holds the Diplome d'Excellence from Maxim's in Paris, and the Grand Diploma from the Cordon Bleu. Now living in Connecticut, Beverly Cox is the author of *Gourmet Minceur, Minceur Italienne*, and the co-author, with Joan Whitman, of *Cooking Techniques*.

Jane Salzfass Freiman

Jane Salzfass Freiman, a Chicago-based cookery instructor for several years, holds a diploma in French culinary arts from Luberon College, in Avignon, France. She has travelled extensively in Italy and is a specialist in Italian cooking. A food writer, she is the author of *The Art of Food Processor Cooking*.

Martha Rose Shulman

Born in Connecticut, Martha Rose Shulman, learned to appreciate many different ethnic foods as a child. She began to cook as a teenager and after college became a professional cook and food writer. Now living in Paris, she is the author of *The Vegetarian Feast* and *Fast Vegetarian Feasts*.

Peter Kump

While he was a college student in Northern California, Peter Kump developed a love of cooking and subsequently studied with many prominent cookery teachers. After moving to New York, he founded the New York Cooking School. Peter Kump is the author of *Quiche and Pâté*.

A Wealth of Herbs

Increasingly, herbs are arriving in the markets fresh; the proliferation of health stores and other specialist shops has widened choice, and many cooks with gardens have taken to raising their own. Recent ethnic influences have called attention to once seemingly esoteric herbs. Coriander, for one, is at last gaining deserved popularity in Europe, although cooks in Asia and the Middle East have been using it for centuries.

Anyone wishing to dry fresh herbs can tie them loosely in a bundle and hang them upside down in a cool, dark, well-ventilated place for several weeks. When the leaves are completely dried, strip them from the stems and store them in an airtight container.

Two swifter methods of preserving herbs make use of the microwave oven and the freezer. To microwave herbs, place five or six sprigs at a time between paper towels and microwave them on high for 1 to 3 minutes until the leaves are brittle. Store the leaves loosely in airtight jars.

To freeze herbs, rinse the sprigs and pat them dry. Strip the leaves off the stems and put them into a heavy-duty plastic bag. Gently flatten the bag to force out the air, seal the bag tightly, and place it in your freezer. Use the leaves as the need arises.

Basil (also called sweet basil): This fragrant herb, with its underlying flavour of anise and hint of clove, goes particularly well with tomato.

Chervil: The small, lacy leaves of this herb have a taste akin to parsley with a touch of anise. It is good in salads and salad dressings. Chervil is popular in France where it is often an ingredient in herb mixtures, including *fines herbes*. When used in cooking, chervil should be added at the end, lest its subtle flavour be lost.

Chives: The smallest of the onions, chives grow in grassy clumps. When finely cut, the hollow leaves contribute their delicate, oniony flavour to fresh salads and raw vegetables. Chives should always be used fresh, as dried ones are virtually tasteless.

Coriander (also called cilantro): The serrated leaves of the coriander plant impart a distinctive fragrance and a flavour that is both mildly sweet and bitter. Coriander leaves should be used fresh or added at the end of cooking if their flavour is to be appreciated fully.

Dill: A sprightly herb with feathery leaves, dill enhances cucumber and many other fresh vegetables, as well as fish and shellfish. When used in cooking, dill should be added towards the end of the process to preserve its delicate flavour. Both dill seeds and dill leaves can be